AF854511

Couples Budgeting

Merge Your Money Without Merging Every Fight About It

Tamsin Blackwell

First edition, 2026

Published by Tamsin Blackwell

Contents

Contents

Chapter 1: The Fight Isn't About the Money

The candle cost forty-seven dollars.

I can still see it sitting on our bookshelf, mocking me. One of those pretentious three-wick things in a heavy glass vessel, the kind that promises to fill your home with "notes of amber and sandalwood" but mostly just smells like expensive wax. My partner bought it without mentioning it. I discovered it when I was putting away groceries and noticed the charge on our shared credit card statement.

We weren't broke. That's what made the whole thing so absurd. We had stable jobs, a comfortable apartment, money in savings. The candle wasn't going to bankrupt us. But when I saw that receipt, something in my chest tightened. Not because of the price tag. Because he hadn't asked. Because in our relationship—this partnership we'd supposedly built on trust and communication—he'd just decided, unilaterally, to spend our money on something I would have considered frivolous.

I didn't say anything at first. I'm not proud of that. I just let it simmer. Every time I walked past that damn candle, unlit and gathering dust, I felt this little spike of resentment. He eventually noticed my mood—hard not to when someone's giving you clipped one-word answers and carefully avoiding eye contact—and asked what was wrong.

"Nothing."

He knew it wasn't nothing.

The fight, when it finally erupted three days later, was spectacular. Not because we were screaming—we don't really do that—but because of how quickly it escalated from a candle to everything else. His defensiveness: "It's just a candle, why are you being so controlling?" My counterattack: "It's not about the candle, it's about respect!" Both of us talking past each other, both of us right and wrong at the same time.

Here's what we were really fighting about, though neither of us could articulate it then: we had never actually discussed what counted as a joint financial decision versus a personal one. We'd moved in together, combined our bank accounts like you're supposed to when you're serious about someone, and assumed that love and good intentions would somehow translate into financial harmony. We'd never set boundaries. Never established a system. Never asked the uncomfortable question of what "ours" actually meant when it came to money.

That candle sat on our shelf for months. A little wax monument to our lack of a system. (I still mess this up sometimes, honestly. Just last week I bought a book without thinking about it, and had to catch myself mid-justification when he glanced at the Amazon box. Old habits.)

I see versions of this fight constantly in my practice. The couples who come to me aren't broke, usually. They're educated professionals with decent incomes and genuine affection for each other. But they're bleeding resentment from a thousand tiny cuts: the subscription service one partner signed up for, the restaurant meal that felt too expensive, the new running shoes that seemed unnecessary, the grocery trip that somehow cost twice the normal amount.

On the surface, it looks like they disagree about money. Dig one layer deeper and you'll find they disagree about priorities—she values experiences, he values security; he thinks $200 on a concert ticket is reasonable, she thinks it's wasteful. But dig deeper still, past the priorities and the purchases, and you hit bedrock: the real issue isn't the money at all. It's power. Control. Respect. The fundamental question of whether you're seen and valued as an individual within the relationship, or whether your autonomy has been quietly absorbed into "us."

The conventional wisdom—the advice you'll find in most personal finance books, the guidance well-meaning friends offer—is that couples should combine everything. Merge those bank accounts. Share credit cards. Become one financial entity. It sounds romantic, doesn't it? Two becoming one. Building a life together. Facing the world as a unified force.

Except in practice, it often plays out more like a hostile takeover.

Think about Melinda and Bill Gates. I know, I know—not exactly a model for relationship success given how things ended. But before the divorce, they were held up as paragraphs of partnership. What's interesting is that even at their level of wealth, even with more money than most of us will see in ten lifetimes, they still had to navigate questions of financial autonomy. Melinda has spoken publicly about how she had to assert herself in philanthropic decisions, how she carved out her own areas of focus within their foundation because otherwise her voice was getting lost in his. If someone with billions of dollars and a legal team needs to establish financial boundaries within a marriage, what makes the rest of us think we can wing it?

Or look at someone like Brené Brown, who's built a career on vulnerability and authentic connection. She's talked about how she and her husband maintain some financial separation—not because they don't trust each other, but because autonomy matters. Because "equal" and "fair" aren't the same thing. Because you can be deeply committed to someone and still need room to make choices that reflect your individual values.

I don't believe in 50/50 splits. I know that's heresy in some circles. People hear that and assume I'm advocating for freeloading or financial irresponsibility. But here's the thing: 50/50 is mathematically equal and emotionally bankrupt. It ignores the reality that people earn different amounts, have different financial obligations from before the relationship, and relate to money in fundamentally different ways based on their personal histories.

When you force a 50/50 split on a couple where one person earns $100,000 and the other earns $45,000, you're not creating fairness. You're creating resentment. The higher earner may feel like they're bankrolling a lifestyle they didn't choose. The lower earner may feel inadequate, guilty, or controlled. Neither of those emotional states is conducive to a healthy relationship.

Proportional contribution—where each person pays into shared expenses based on their income—is the only approach that actually respects both partners' autonomy while acknowledging reality. If you earn 60% of the household income, you contribute 60% to shared costs. Your partner contributes 40%. This isn't complicated math, but it requires something much harder than math: it requires letting go of the idea that "equal" is the same as "fair."

I worked with a couple once, Sarah and Marcus, who were drowning in resentment over this exact issue. Sarah was a software engineer pulling in about $140,000 a year. Marcus was a high school teacher making $52,000. They'd been together for four years, living together for two, and splitting everything exactly down the middle because that's what seemed "fair."

Except Marcus was barely scraping by. After contributing his half of rent, utilities, and groceries, he had almost nothing left for savings

or personal spending. Meanwhile Sarah had plenty of cushion in her budget. She'd suggest they go out to dinner or take a weekend trip, he'd agree because he didn't want to seem cheap or hold her back, and then he'd spend the next week stressed about his credit card balance. She'd offer to pay, he'd refuse because that felt like charity. They were trapped in this horrible cycle where every financial decision was fraught with unspoken tension.

When I suggested proportional contribution, Marcus actually teared up. Not because it was revolutionary—the math is simple enough that he'd probably thought of it himself—but because Sarah immediately agreed. She'd been wanting to suggest something similar for months but was afraid it would seem condescending or like she was trying to hold financial power over him. They'd both been silently suffering rather than risk the vulnerability of the conversation.

Here's what kills me: they loved each other. Genuinely, deeply. They were kind people who wanted the best for each other. But they'd been operating under a system that was slowly poisoning their relationship, and they couldn't see a way out because the conventional wisdom said 50/50 was the only "fair" approach.

We restructured everything. Sarah started contributing 65% to their shared expenses, Marcus 35%—roughly proportional to their incomes. Suddenly Marcus could breathe. He could save money. He could make a spontaneous purchase without calculating whether it would wreck his budget. And Sarah didn't feel like she was carrying the relationship financially—because the system itself acknowledged reality rather than forcing them into an arbitrary standard of "equality."

But proportional contribution alone isn't enough. You also need boundaries. You need designated spaces where each person maintains autonomy. That's where the three-account system comes in: Yours, Mine, Ours.

The "Mine" account is non-negotiable personal money. Your space to make choices that reflect your values without justification or approval. For some people that's coffee shops and books. For others it's vinyl records or art supplies or weekend rock climbing trips. The specific spending doesn't matter; what matters is that it's yours. Completely, unambiguously yours.

I learned this the hard way, obviously. That candle fight was really about the fact that my partner and I had never established what "personal spending" meant in our relationship. We'd combined our finances but never carved out individual territory. So every purchase felt like it needed to be defensible, like it was being taken from some shared pool that we both had veto power over.

Once we established separate "Mine" accounts—a set amount each month that was ours to spend without discussion—the tension evaporated. I'm not exaggerating. Within weeks, the low-level financial bickering that had become background noise in our relationship just... stopped. Not because our priorities suddenly aligned, but because we'd created a structure that respected our differences.

The "Ours" account is for shared expenses: rent or mortgage, utilities, groceries, insurance, savings goals you've agreed on together. This is the practical infrastructure of your shared life. Everything that benefits you both equally goes here. And critically, you contribute to this account proportionally based on income—not 50/50 unless you happen to earn exactly the same amount, which almost no one does.

The "Yours" account—and this is where people often get confused—is for individual financial obligations that existed before the relationship. Student loans from that graduate degree you got five years before you met your partner. The car payment on the vehicle you bought when you were single. Credit card debt from your twenties. These are your responsibilities, not shared burdens.

I know some people bristle at this. They think true partnership means taking on everything together, that keeping student loans separate is somehow holding back or not fully committing. But consider what happens when you don't maintain that boundary: one person's pre-existing debt becomes a shared financial drain that breeds resentment. The person who came into the relationship debt-free starts to feel penalized for their earlier financial responsibility. The person with debt feels guilty and inadequate. Neither of those emotional states strengthens your relationship.

Take Jordan and Alex. Jordan had about $60,000 in student loans from law school. Alex had none—had gone to a state school on scholarship and graduated debt-free. When they got married, they combined everything, including Jordan's loan payments. For the first year, Alex didn't think much about it. They were a team. They'd tackle it together.

But as the years went on and that monthly $800 payment kept getting deducted from their shared account, Alex started feeling something he couldn't quite name at first. Not resentment exactly, but a kind of background irritation. When they'd talk about buying a house or taking a big vacation, Jordan's loans were always this limiting factor. Alex found himself thinking things he wasn't proud of: "If we didn't have these payments, we could..." or "I didn't even go to law school, why am I paying for it?"

Meanwhile Jordan felt horrible. Every loan payment felt like a referendum on his worth. He'd apologize for the debt, Alex would insist it was fine, and neither of them was being fully honest about how it was affecting them.

When they restructured so Jordan's loan payments came from his individual account—his "Yours" money—the dynamic shifted. Yes, it meant Jordan had less discretionary spending than Alex after all obligations were met. But that felt fair to both of them in a way the previous system hadn't. Jordan wasn't burdening Alex with his pre-relationship choices. Alex wasn't subsidizing a decision he'd had no part in making. They could focus on building their shared future rather than relitigating the past.

None of this works, though, without the hard part: actually having the conversation. And I mean the real conversation, not the surface-level "we should probably talk about money sometime" discussion that you have once and then consider handled. I mean the ongoing, sometimes uncomfortable, occasionally vulnerable dialogue about what money means to each of you.

You have to be willing to talk about your financial fears. The ones that feel embarrassing or irrational. Like how spending money on yourself makes you feel guilty because your mom always called that selfish. Or how watching your partner spend freely triggers something from when your dad lost his job and your family almost lost the house. Or how you feel less-than because you earn less, even though intellectually you know your work has value.

These aren't rational financial decisions. They're emotional landmines left over from childhood, from past relationships, from cultural messages about worth and responsibility and what it means to be a good partner. You can have the perfect budget spreadsheet and it won't matter if you haven't excavated that emotional foundation.

I remember working with a couple—I'll call them Rachel and Tom—who could not stop fighting about groceries. Sounds absurd, right? But every shopping trip became a battle. Rachel would buy organic produce, grass-fed meat, fancy cheese. Tom would see the receipt and lose his mind. They made good money, the grocery bill wasn't actually straining their budget, but Tom would get genuinely angry about the "waste."

After a few sessions, the real story emerged. Tom had grown up poor. Like, electricity-getting-shut-off poor. His mom had stretched every dollar, bought dented cans from the discount rack, watered down juice to make it last longer. Spending $7 on a wedge of cheese when you could get a block for $3 wasn't frugal to him—it was a moral failing. It meant you'd forgotten where you came from.

Rachel, meanwhile, had grown up solidly middle class. Not wealthy, but comfortable. To her, buying quality food was basic self-care. It wasn't extravagant; it was normal. She couldn't understand why Tom was policing her grocery choices like they were on the verge of bankruptcy.

Neither of them was wrong. But they were operating from completely different frameworks shaped by completely different experiences, and they'd never actually talked about it. Once they did—once Tom could articulate why grocery spending triggered such anxiety, and Rachel could understand that it wasn't about her personally—they could find a compromise. They set a grocery budget that felt reasonable to both of them, with wiggle room for Rachel to buy the items that mattered to her and boundaries that helped Tom feel secure.

This is the work. Not the spreadsheets and apps, though those can be useful tools. The actual work is excavating your money stories, making them visible to your partner, and creating a system that honors both people's emotional realities while still functioning practically.

Start simple. Don't try to architect the perfect financial system on day one. Begin with three questions:

What do you need to feel financially secure in this relationship?

What do you need to feel financially autonomous?

Where are you willing to compromise?

Your answers will be different from your partner's. That's not a problem to be solved; it's information to be integrated. Maybe you need to see a certain amount in savings before you can relax. Maybe your partner needs permission to spend on hobbies without justification. Maybe you both need clearer boundaries around what constitutes a joint decision versus an individual one.

From there, you can build out the practical structure. Calculate your combined income. List your shared expenses. Determine proportional contributions. Agree on an amount for individual "Mine" accounts. Decide how to handle pre-existing individual debts. Set a threshold for what size purchase requires discussion—maybe anything over $100, maybe over $500, whatever feels right for your situation.

Then live with it for a month. See what works and what doesn't. Adjust. Keep talking. This isn't a one-time fix; it's an ongoing calibration. Your incomes will change. Your priorities will shift. Life will throw you curveballs—job loss, medical expenses, family emergencies. The system you build needs to be flexible enough to accommodate reality.

And here's the thing I wish someone had told me earlier, before the candle fight and months of simmering resentment: creating financial boundaries isn't a sign of mistrust or lack of commitment. It's the opposite. It's saying "I trust you enough to be honest about my needs" and "I respect you enough to honor yours." It's building a relationship where both people can thrive as individuals while also functioning as a partnership.

Because here's what I've learned, both professionally and from my own stumbling progress with my partner: the couples who make it aren't the ones who never fight about money. They're the ones who've learned to fight productively. Who can name their fears and needs without shame. Who've built systems that create space for both togetherness and autonomy. Who understand that financial harmony isn't about agreeing on everything—it's about respecting each other enough to make room for disagreement.

The fight was never about the candle. It was about whether I felt seen and respected within our financial partnership. Whether my input mattered. Whether "ours" meant we were building something together or whether it meant my individual needs had been absorbed into some amorphous shared entity where I'd lost my voice.

Your fight probably isn't about money either. It's about what the money represents: security, control, worth, respect, autonomy, trust. And once you can name what you're really fighting about—once you can move past the candle or the shoes or the grocery bill to the deeper need underneath—you can start building something that actually works. Not a perfect system, because those don't exist. But one that honors both of you. One that creates room for both shared goals and individual expression. One where you can buy a candle if you want to, or not, and either way it's just a candle instead of a symbol of everything wrong with your relationship.

Which brings us to the practical question you're probably asking: how do you actually start this conversation with your partner without it turning into the very fight you're trying to avoid?

Chapter 2: The 'Mine' Account: Protecting Your Financial Identity

I was standing in Target when my phone buzzed. A text from my wife: "Did you just spend $47 at Barnes & Noble?"

We'd been married three years. We had a joint checking account, shared credit cards, a meticulously color-coded spreadsheet tracking every dollar. We were doing everything right, or so I thought. And yet here I was, frozen between the paper towels and the laundry detergent, feeling like I'd been caught stealing from my own life.

I'd bought three books. That's it. Three paperbacks I'd been wanting to read for months. And now I was supposed to... what? Apologize? Explain myself? Justify why I spent money I'd earned on something I wanted?

I typed back: "Yeah, just some books." Then I deleted it. Tried again: "Yep, got a few things for myself." Delete. Finally settled on: "Yeah, why?"

Her response: "Just wondering. Saw the notification."

Just wondering. Two words that meant: I'm watching. I'm tracking. I'm keeping tabs.

That night, I didn't bring the books inside. Left them in my car for two days before I worked up the nerve to carry them in. And I still remember thinking: this is insane. We make good money. We're not struggling. Why does buying three books feel like a crime?

Here's what I didn't understand then: the problem wasn't the money. It was that I'd lost something fundamental when we merged our finances—the ability to make a decision, even a small one, without invisible surveillance. My wife wasn't trying to control me (though it felt that way). She was just doing what we'd agreed to do: monitor our spending, stay accountable, build something together.

But "together" had somehow become "under scrutiny." And I guarantee you, if you're reading this, one of you has felt exactly what I felt standing in that Target. Maybe both of you have.

This is why the "mine" account isn't optional. It's not a luxury for couples who have money left over after covering the basics. It's the foundation that makes everything else possible. Skip this step and you're building your financial life on a fault line—it might hold for a while, but eventually something's going to crack.

Let me say something that's going to sound counterintuitive: I don't believe in equal. I believe in fair. And those two things are almost never the same.

The standard couples' finance advice—split everything 50/50, contribute equally, share the burden—sounds beautiful in theory. In practice? It's a setup for resentment. Because equal contributions only work if both partners earn exactly the same amount, have exactly the same spending habits, and value exactly the same things. Show me a couple where that's true and I'll show you... well, I'll show you nobody, because that couple doesn't exist.

Sarah makes $85,000 a year working in tech. Her husband David teaches high school and brings home $48,000. They kept separate finances for the first year of marriage because they couldn't agree on how to merge them. Sarah wanted to split everything down the middle—"We're equal partners, we should contribute equally." David agreed in principle but the math made him sweat. Splitting rent ($2,400), utilities ($300), groceries ($600), and insurance ($400) meant he was putting $1,850 toward household expenses every month while Sarah put in the same amount. On paper: fair. In reality: David had $1,150 left for everything else in his life—car payment, gas, phone, student loans, any personal spending. Sarah had $4,950.

David started declining dinner invitations. Stopped buying new clothes. Skipped his sister's destination wedding because he couldn't afford the flight. Meanwhile Sarah was building savings, maxing out her 401k, booking weekend trips. The resentment built slowly, like water behind a dam. He felt poor in his own marriage. She felt guilty for succeeding. Neither of them talked about it until David finally exploded one night: "I can't afford to be your equal partner."

That's when they found proportional contribution. Instead of splitting expenses 50/50, they split them based on income ratio. Sarah earned roughly 64% of their combined income, David earned 36%. So Sarah covered 64% of shared expenses ($2,176) and David covered 36% ($1,224). Suddenly David had $2,776 left over instead of $1,150. Sarah still had $4,824—less than before, but hardly a hardship. More importantly: they both had breathing room. They both felt like partners instead of roommates trapped in a bad lease.

This is the hill I'll die on: proportional contribution is the only approach that respects both partners' autonomy while acknowledging that mathematical equality and actual fairness are different things. You wouldn't ask someone in a wheelchair to take the stairs just because that's what you're doing. So why ask someone earning $48,000 to contribute the same dollar amount as someone earning $85,000?

(I still mess this up sometimes, by the way. Last year my income jumped and I kept calculating our split based on the old numbers for three months because change is hard and doing math is annoying. My wife finally sat me down with a calculator and we recalibrated. The system only works if you actually use it.)

Now, once you've figured out proportional contribution to shared expenses, you're left with whatever remains. This is where most couples make their second mistake: they treat that remaining money as "ours" by default. Everything goes into the joint account. Every purchase becomes a committee decision. Every dollar is accounted for, tracked, justified.

And that's how you end up texting your spouse about $47 at Barnes & Noble.

The "mine" account—truly yours, no questions asked, no justification required—isn't about hiding purchases or keeping secrets. It's about preserving the part of yourself that existed before "we" became the default pronoun for every financial decision. You had a life before this relationship. You had interests, hobbies, quirks, small pleasures that didn't require a financial committee meeting. The "mine" account says: that person still exists, and still deserves space.

I'm not talking about huge sums here. The amount almost doesn't matter. I've seen this work with couples setting aside $100 a month per person, and I've seen it work with couples setting aside $1,000. What matters is the principle: this money is mine, full stop. I don't have to explain why I bought another book when I haven't finished the stack on my nightstand. You don't have to justify your third pair of running shoes this year. We get to be a little irrational, a little impulsive, a little human—without the relationship paying the price.

Here's how to actually set this up. Calculate your net monthly income—what hits your bank account after taxes, insurance, retirement contributions, all the stuff that gets pulled out before you see it. Let's say you bring home $4,200 and your partner brings home $3,100. Combined: $7,300.

Start with 10% as your baseline. That means $420 goes into your "mine" account every month, $310 goes into theirs. You can adjust this up or down based on your financial situation—maybe you start at 5% because money's tight, or maybe you go to 15% because you've got room and you value that autonomy. The percentage matters less than the consistency. This isn't bonus money when times are good. It's a line item in your budget, as non-negotiable as rent.

And then—this is the part that feels weird at first—you don't track what the other person does with it. You don't comment. You don't raise your eyebrows when packages arrive. You definitely don't text them asking why they spent $47 at Barnes & Noble.

Maria and Alex did this and it saved their marriage. Not exaggerating. They'd been together eight years, married for four, and they were thisclose to separating when they came to see me. The presenting issue was "financial incompatibility." Maria said Alex was irresponsible with money. Alex said Maria was controlling. What it actually was: they'd merged everything, and Maria's natural tendency to track and plan had turned into surveillance. Every time Alex bought lunch instead of packing one, Maria saw it. Every time he grabbed a beer with friends, she knew. He felt suffocated. She felt like she was the only adult in the relationship.

I had them set up "mine" accounts—15% of net income each. For Maria that was $615 a month. For Alex, $480. The rule: no commentary on how the other person spent it. None. If Alex wanted to blow his entire $480 on craft beer and vintage vinyl records, that was his call. If Maria wanted to save hers for three months and book a solo weekend at a spa, that was hers.

The first month was rough. Maria kept catching herself checking Alex's account balance. Alex felt guilty every time he spent money and would preemptively explain himself. But by month three something had shifted. Alex started a monthly poker game with friends—his buy-in came from his "mine" account, so Maria never saw it, never commented, never made him feel like he was choosing poker over their future. Maria booked pottery classes she'd been wanting to take for years but had felt too guilty to spend "their" money on.

Here's what surprised them: they actually started talking about money more, not less. Because when they did discuss shared spending—vacations, furniture, home repairs—there was no undercurrent of resentment. Alex wasn't thinking "She tracks every dollar I spend, why does she get to propose a $2,000 couch?" Maria wasn't thinking "He can't even pack a lunch, how can I trust him with a big purchase?" They'd each had space to be themselves, independently, which made collaboration on shared goals feel like actual partnership instead of surrender.

Six months in, they both told me the same thing: the "mine" account felt like getting permission to be human. To be imperfect. To want things that didn't make sense to anyone else but made perfect sense to them.

You're probably thinking: okay, but what if my partner wastes their "mine" money? What if they blow it on stupid stuff?

First, define "stupid stuff." Because I'm willing to bet what looks like waste to you is actually something your partner values deeply. My wife spends money on plants. We have maybe forty houseplants at this point, which from my perspective is approximately thirty-eight too many. Does she need another pothos? Objectively, no. Does it bring her genuine joy to propagate cuttings and arrange them in weird vintage containers? Yes. So it's not waste. It's just not something I value the same way.

Second—and this is harder to accept—part of the point is letting each other make mistakes. Maybe your partner does spend $300 on something genuinely useless. Maybe it sits in the closet for six months and then gets donated. That's... okay? That's how people learn. You don't build financial wisdom by outsourcing every decision to a committee. You build it by trying things, screwing up occasionally, and adjusting. The "mine" account is the training ground for that. The stakes are low because it's a contained amount. But the lessons are real.

That said, if one partner is consistently overspending their "mine" account and dipping into shared funds to cover it, you've got a bigger problem. The "mine" account only works if both people respect the boundaries. It's not a free-for-all. It's freedom within a framework.

I watched this play out with Jake and Ben. They set up "mine" accounts—$500 each per month. Within two months, Jake had racked up an extra $800 in personal spending beyond his allocation. He'd put it on a credit card, figuring he'd pay it off later. Ben found out when he checked their credit card statement and saw charges from a golf simulator rental, a high-end whiskey subscription, and a $300 set of poker chips. He was furious—not because of the purchases themselves, but because Jake had broken the one rule: stay within your "mine" budget.

They had the fight. Jake's position: "It's my money, I earned it, why do I need permission?" Ben's position: "We agreed on $500. Going $800 over affects both of us because now that's $800 we don't have for shared goals."

They were both right and both wrong. The resolution: they revisited the allocation. Turned out $500 wasn't enough for Jake's actual spending patterns—he'd been spending closer to $900 a month on personal stuff before they got together. They looked at the budget and found room to increase his "mine" account to $700. In exchange, Jake committed to hard boundaries: once the $700 was gone, it was gone. No credit card backup. No dipping into shared funds. It worked because they both gave something up—Ben gave up the lower number, Jake gave up the flexibility to overspend.

Let me give you a framework you can actually use tonight. Sit down with your partner—literally, right now if you can—and work through this together.

Step one: Calculate each person's net monthly income. This is after taxes, after insurance, after retirement contributions—what actually lands in your account. Write it down.

Partner A: $__________ **Partner B: $__________**

Step two: Add those together. That's your household income.

Combined: $__________

Step three: Calculate your income ratio. Divide each person's income by the combined total. This is the percentage each of you contributes to shared expenses.

Partner A percentage: ________% **Partner B percentage: ________%**

Step four: List your shared monthly expenses. Be thorough: rent or mortgage, utilities, groceries, insurance, minimum debt payments, streaming services you both use, whatever genuinely benefits both of you.

Total shared expenses: $__________

Step five: Multiply your total shared expenses by each person's percentage. That's how much each of you contributes to the joint account.

Partner A contributes: $__________ **Partner B contributes: $__________**

Step six: Subtract each person's contribution from their net income. What's left is discretionary money.

Partner A remaining: $__________ **Partner B remaining: $__________**

Step seven: Decide what percentage of that remaining money goes into each person's "mine" account. Start with 10% if you're not sure. This money is untouchable by the other person, no questions asked.

Partner A "mine" account: $__________ **Partner B "mine" account: $__________**

Step eight: Automate it. Set up automatic transfers on payday. Partner A's income lands, and immediately $X goes to the joint account for shared expenses, $Y goes to the "mine" account, and whatever's left stays in their personal checking for individual expenses that aren't covered by the "mine" budget (think: gas, work lunches, personal phone bill).

Step nine: Establish one rule and one rule only for the "mine" account: we don't comment on how the other person spends it. We don't judge, we don't track, we don't investigate. It's yours. It's mine. Full stop.

This is going to feel strange at first, especially if you've been operating with fully merged finances. It might even feel like a step backward—wait, I thought we were building a life together, why are we splitting things up?

Because autonomy isn't the opposite of partnership. It's the foundation.

Think about friendships for a second. You probably have individual friends your partner doesn't hang out with. Maybe you grab lunch with a coworker once a week, or you've got a group chat with college friends your partner isn't part of. Does that threaten your relationship? No. It makes you a more complete person, which makes you a better partner. Same principle applies to money.

When my wife and I finally set up "mine" accounts—years after that Barnes & Noble incident, way later than we should have—the first thing I bought was a guitar. I'd been wanting one for probably a decade. But it felt frivolous, you know? We were saving for a house. We had student loans. A guitar wasn't a priority. Except every time I passed a music store, I'd pause. Look in the window. Walk away.

I saved my "mine" money for four months and bought a used Martin for $650. I didn't ask permission. I didn't justify it. I just... bought it. And when I brought it home, my wife didn't interrogate me about whether we could afford it or whether I'd actually stick with lessons. She said, "Oh cool, what kind is it?"

That guitar is still in our living room. I'm not very good—I practice maybe twice a week, and I'll never be more than a mediocre hobbyist. But every time I play it, I remember: I get to want things that don't make financial sense. I get to be a little impractical. I get to be myself, not just the responsible half of a financial partnership.

Your "mine" account might buy you a guitar. It might buy you monthly massages, or a gym membership, or donations to causes your partner doesn't care about, or a savings fund for something you can't even name yet. It doesn't matter what it buys. What matters is the permission it gives you: to remain an individual inside a partnership.

One more thing before we move on, because I know this question is coming: what about big purchases?

The "mine" account works great for the $47 Barnes & Noble run, the monthly subscription boxes, the occasional splurge at Target. But what about the $2,000 mountain bike, or the $5,000 photography course, or the $10,000 car your partner wants to buy without consulting you?

Here's the boundary: if it's going to take you six months or more to save up for it from your "mine" account, you talk about it first. Not to ask permission, but to give your partner context. "Hey, I'm planning to save my 'mine' money for the next eight months to buy a road bike. Just wanted you to know that's where that money's going."

That way they're not blindsided when a $2,500 purchase suddenly appears. And it gives you both a chance to think about whether there are shared funds that could contribute—maybe this is something that benefits both of you, or maybe it's purely individual, but at least you're on the same page.

Transparency within boundaries. That's the sweet spot.

Lisa and Mark hit this exact scenario. Mark's a woodworker—I mean a serious one, the kind of guy who can tell you the grain pattern of walnut versus cherry just by looking. He'd been eyeing a vintage table saw for months, watching listings, waiting for the right one to pop up. When it finally did, the price was $3,200. He had $1,800 saved in his "mine" account. He could've just put the difference on a credit card and dealt with it later. Instead, he told Lisa: "I found the saw. I'm $1,400 short. I can wait and save up, or I can pull from our joint savings and pay it back over the next few months. What do you think?"

Lisa appreciated the heads-up. They talked through it. The joint savings was earmarked for a vacation fund, but they weren't planning to book anything for another six months. They agreed Mark could borrow the $1,400, pay it back at $350 a month from his "mine" account, and they'd still hit their vacation goal on time. Mark got his saw. Lisa didn't feel ambushed. The relationship survived a $3,200 purchase that could've easily turned into a weeklong fight.

This is the thing nobody tells you about money in relationships: the dollar amount of a purchase is almost never the actual problem. The problem is feeling blindsided, or disrespected, or like your input doesn't matter. The "mine" account fixes that by creating clear expectations. Below a certain threshold: your call, no discussion needed. Above that threshold: give me context so I'm not surprised.

You'll have to decide what that threshold is for yourselves. For some couples it's $200. For others it's $1,000. Pick a number that reflects your financial reality and your comfort level with independent decision-making, and then revisit it every six months to see if it still makes sense.

Here's what I wish someone had told me fifteen years ago, back when I was hiding books in my car: money is never just about money.

When you fight about the $47 at Barnes & Noble, you're not actually fighting about forty-seven dollars. You're fighting about trust, autonomy, respect, fear of scarcity, childhood messages about worthiness, control, partnership, whether you're allowed to want things that don't serve the collective good. That's a lot of weight for three paperbacks to carry.

The "mine" account doesn't solve all of that. But it takes the pressure off. It gives you a space where the answer to "Can I buy this?" is always yes, as long as you're within budget. And that automatic yes—that freedom from justification—clears room for the real conversations. The ones about what you actually value, what your shared future looks like, what you're building together and what you're building separately.

Sarah and David, the couple from earlier with the income disparity? They've been using proportional contribution and "mine" accounts for three years now. Sarah told me something recently that stuck with me. She said, "I used to think the goal was to merge everything—combine our money, combine our goals, become one financial unit. Now I think the goal is to build something together while staying whole separately. The 'mine' account reminded me that David's a complete person, not just my partner. He had a whole life before me. He'll have a whole life if I get hit by a bus tomorrow. The least I can do is let him spend $300 a month however he wants."

That's it. That's the whole point. You're not trying to erase yourself to become "we." You're trying to figure out how two complete, complicated, occasionally irrational humans can build a shared life without losing the individual ones.

The "mine" account is where you practice that balance. Three hundred dollars a month, five hundred, whatever number you land on—it's not about the amount. It's about drawing a line and saying: this part's mine, that part's yours, and everything else is ours. And somehow, paradoxically, those clear boundaries make the "ours" part stronger.

So maybe grab your partner tonight. Pull out that framework from earlier. Calculate your ratios, figure out your allocations, set up the automatic transfers. Give yourselves permission to be individuals inside this partnership. And then—this is the hard part—actually let each other use that money without commentary.

Your partner might buy something you think is ridiculous. That's fine. They might waste a month's allocation on something that ends up in the donation pile by next year. Also fine. They might surprise you and save it for six months to fund something beautiful you never would've thought of. Even better.

What you're building here isn't just a budgeting system. You're building the architecture of a relationship where both people get to be fully themselves and fully committed at the same time. Where you can text your partner about a $47 purchase not because you need permission, but because you're excited about what you bought and want to share it with them.

That's the relationship on the other side of this. The one where money stops being a battleground and starts being a tool. Where you stop tracking each other's purchases and start trusting each other's judgment. Where "mine" and "yours" and "ours" all have space to exist, and the boundaries between them make everything clearer instead of more complicated.

We'll talk about the "ours" account next—the shared pool where proportional contribution really proves its worth. But first you need this foundation. You need to know that even inside a committed partnership, you still get to be you. The "mine" account is how you prove it.

Chapter 3: The 'Ours' Account: Shared Responsibilities, Proportional Contributions

I'm going to be honest with you: I believed in 50/50 splits for the first eight years of my relationship. Genuinely believed in them. It felt like the only adult, fair way to handle money with a partner. Equal. Clean. Nobody gets taken advantage of.

Then my income doubled in a single year.

I was a freelance writer who'd been scraping by on $45,000 annually when a consulting contract landed in my lap—steady work, actual health insurance, $95,000 salary. My partner was (and still is) a high school art teacher making $52,000. We'd been splitting rent, utilities, groceries straight down the middle for nearly a decade. $1,400 each for rent. $150 each for electric and gas. We had a whole Google Sheet.

That first month after my raise, I watched him transfer his half of the rent, and something in my chest went tight. He was contributing the same dollar amount as me, but I was suddenly sitting on an extra $3,000 a month after taxes while he... wasn't. His "half" was eating up a drastically larger portion of his paycheck than mine. The math that had felt so fair for years now felt—I don't know how else to say this—kind of cruel.

We kept the system for three more months. I didn't say anything because I didn't know *what* to say. Asking him to pay less felt patronizing, like I was offering charity. But watching him stress about a $200 car repair while I casually ordered takeout twice a week made me feel complicit in something fundamentally unfair.

Here's what I wish someone had told me then: equal contribution and fair contribution are not the same thing. Not even close.

A 50/50 split works beautifully when two people earn roughly the same amount and have similar financial obligations. It falls apart—slowly, poisonously—when income is lopsided. The lower earner feels broke while contributing their "fair share." The higher earner feels weird about their excess. Nobody talks about it because the system is *technically* equitable, so what's there to complain about?

Everything, actually.

This is the unspoken cost of the 50/50 default: it turns money into a source of quiet, grinding resentment instead of a tool you use together. The higher earner starts to feel like they're subsidizing a lifestyle they're not even enjoying—why are we splitting this tiny grocery budget when I could easily cover the organic stuff I actually want? The lower earner starts to feel financially stuck, unable to save or spend freely because "their half" of shared expenses is consuming too much of their income. You're roommates with a shared bathroom, not partners building something.

I've watched this play out in dozens of relationships. A couple I know—let's call them Rachel and Matt—split everything 50/50 for six years. Rachel worked in tech and cleared $140,000. Matt was a social worker making $48,000. They paid $1,850 each in rent, $200 each for groceries, $100 each for utilities. Rachel barely noticed these expenses. Matt was perpetually stretched thin, unable to save, skipping dinners out with friends because he'd already allocated his "half" to the household.

Rachel started to resent that she couldn't suggest nicer things—a better apartment, a weekend trip, a meal-kit subscription—because

Matt couldn't afford his half. Matt resented that Rachel seemed to have infinite disposable income while he was counting days until payday. Neither of them was *wrong*. The system was wrong.

The 50/50 split pretends that fairness is a math equation. It's not. Fairness is about proportional sacrifice.

Let me back up.

When I finally sat down with my partner and said, "I think we need to change how we're splitting expenses," I didn't have a plan. I had a feeling—that sick, knotted feeling you get when something is structurally off and you've been ignoring it because you don't know how to fix it. We spent two hours at the kitchen table with a calculator and a bottle of wine, trying to figure out what "fair" even meant if it wasn't 50/50.

What we landed on—and what I'm going to walk you through now—is proportional contribution. It sounds technical. It's not. It's just this: each person contributes to shared expenses based on their percentage of the household income, not a flat dollar amount.

Here's the actual math. My partner and I bring home a combined $12,000 per month after taxes (my $7,900 + his $4,100). I earn about 66% of that total. He earns 34%. So instead of splitting our $3,200 in shared monthly expenses down the middle ($1,600 each), I contribute 66%—about $2,112—and he contributes 34%, roughly $1,088.

That's it. That's the whole system.

It shifts the frame from *equal amounts* to *equal burden*. I'm not paying "more than my fair share"—I'm paying a share that reflects my income. He's not "getting away with less"—he's contributing what's proportional to what he earns. We're both sacrificing a comparable percentage of our financial capacity for the household we share.

The relief was immediate. Not just financial relief—emotional relief. We stopped having those weird, unspoken tensions about money. I could suggest we upgrade our internet plan or buy the nicer coffee beans without worrying it would strain his budget. He could save for a new camera lens without feeling like he was failing at his share of the bills. We were suddenly on the same team again.

(I still mess this up sometimes, by the way. Last year I forgot we'd agreed to reassess our percentages after my partner got a small raise, and I kept auto-transferring the old amount for three months before he gently reminded me. The system isn't magic. It just makes the baseline fairer so when you *do* mess up, it's a fixable mistake instead of a festering resentment.)

Let's talk about what actually goes into this shared pool—the "Ours" account.

This is where couples often get tangled up, because the instinct is to lump *everything* together or keep *everything* separate, and neither extreme works. You need a clear boundary: what counts as a shared responsibility, and what stays individual?

Start with the non-negotiables. Housing costs—rent or mortgage, property taxes, insurance. Utilities—electric, gas, water, trash, internet. These aren't luxuries. They're the infrastructure of your shared life. They go in the "Ours" bucket.

Groceries usually belong here too, though I'll add a caveat: if one person does 90% of the cooking and meal planning, it's worth acknowledging that labor when you're talking about contributions. Maybe the person doing less cooking picks up a slightly higher percentage of the grocery cost, or maybe they take on a different household expense to balance it out. The point isn't rigid formulas—it's agreeing on what feels equitable to both of you.

Transportation gets murkier. If you share a car, the costs—loan payment, insurance, gas, maintenance—are shared. If you each have your own car and commute separately, those expenses stay individual. If one of you takes public transit and the other drives, the transit pass might be individual, or it might be shared if you both use it regularly for errands. There's no universal rule here. You're drawing a line together.

The real question is this: does this expense benefit both of us roughly equally, and is it essential to our household? If yes, it's shared. If no—if it's discretionary, or if it disproportionately benefits one person—it stays in individual budgets.

Streaming services are a good test case. If you both watch Netflix, it's shared. If one person has a Criterion Channel subscription and the other never touches it, that's individual. Gym memberships, same logic. Dining out? That's typically individual unless you explicitly agree to treat it as a shared "date night" budget.

Here's the thing nobody tells you: you're going to get some of these categorizations wrong at first. That's fine. My partner and I initially put our pet expenses in the "Ours" account because we adopted the dog together. Six months in, I realized I was the one doing 100% of the vet visits, grooming appointments, and food runs, and it started to feel less like a shared responsibility and more like... my dog. We moved pet costs to my individual budget and rebalanced our percentages slightly. No drama. Just adjustment.

The framework isn't about getting it perfect on the first try. It's about having a system flexible enough to adapt as your lives change.

Now let's talk about the actual calculation, because this is where people's eyes glaze over and they default back to 50/50 because "it's easier." It's not easier. It's *simpler*, which is different. Simpler math doesn't mean less resentment.

Here's how you calculate proportional contributions. Step one: Figure out each person's monthly take-home income after taxes and deductions. Not gross salary—actual money hitting your account. Let's say Partner A brings home $5,000/month and Partner B brings home $3,000/month.

Step two: Add those together. Combined monthly income is $8,000.

Step three: Calculate each person's percentage of that total. Partner A is earning $5,000 out of $8,000, which is 62.5%. Partner B is earning $3,000 out of $8,000, or 37.5%.

Step four: Apply those percentages to your shared expenses. If your "Ours" budget is $2,400/month (rent, utilities, groceries, etc.), Partner A contributes 62.5% of that—$1,500—and Partner B contributes 37.5%, or $900.

That's the whole formula. You can set it up as an automatic transfer on payday so nobody has to think about it month to month. The money just flows into a joint account earmarked for shared expenses, and you pay your household bills from there.

What I love about this system—and I mean *love*, which is a weird thing to say about a budgeting method, but here we are—is that it auto-adjusts when income changes. If Partner A gets a raise and their monthly income jumps to $6,000, the combined total is now $9,000. Partner A's percentage increases to 66.7%, and Partner B's drops to 33.3%. Next month, Partner A contributes $1,600 to the

$2,400 budget, and Partner B contributes $800.

Nobody has to renegotiate. Nobody has to feel guilty. The system flexibly reflects your current financial reality.

Let me show you what this looks like in practice.

Take Emily and Ben. Emily's a public school teacher earning $55,000 a year—about $3,800/month after taxes and insurance. Ben's a freelance photographer whose income bounces around, but he averages $42,000 annually, or roughly $3,000/month. Combined, they're bringing in $6,800/month.

Emily earns 56% of that total. Ben earns 44%.

Their shared expenses look like this: $1,650 rent, $180 utilities, $500 groceries, $120 internet and streaming services, $200 car insurance (shared vehicle). Total: $2,650/month.

Using proportional contributions, Emily pays $1,484 (56% of $2,650) and Ben pays $1,166 (44%). They each set up an automatic transfer from their individual checking accounts into a joint account on the first of the month. Bills get paid from there. Done.

Here's what happens when Ben has a fantastic month and books a $6,000 wedding shoot, bumping his annual average up to $50,000 ($3,600/month). Now their combined income is $7,400. Emily's percentage drops to 51%, and Ben's rises to 49%. The following month, Emily contributes $1,351 to the shared expenses and Ben contributes $1,299.

Ben's not being punished for earning more. Emily's not being penalized for staying at the same income. The burden just redistributes to match the new reality.

This took me three years to fully understand, by the way—not the math, but the *philosophy*. I kept thinking of it as "the higher earner pays more," which made it feel lopsided. What finally clicked: we're not paying *more*. We're paying a proportional share of our capacity. Someone earning $8,000/month contributing $2,000 to shared expenses has $6,000 left. Someone earning $4,000/month contributing $1,000 has $3,000 left. Same ratio. Different amounts, same burden.

That's fairness.

One more thing about the "Ours" account itself: keep it simple. It's a joint checking account that exists solely for shared expenses. Not savings. Not discretionary spending. Just the recurring monthly costs you've both agreed are collective responsibilities. You can open it at your current bank or use an online-only account with no fees—doesn't matter. What matters is that it's transparent, easily accessible to both of you, and used exclusively for its designated purpose.

Some couples get fancy with this and create sub-accounts for different categories of shared spending—one for housing, one for groceries, one for transportation. I think that's overkill for most people, but if you're the kind of person who loves that level of organization, go for it. The tool doesn't matter. The principle does.

And here's the principle distilled: shared expenses are funded proportionally based on income, so both partners carry an equivalent financial load relative to what they earn. You're building a system where nobody feels taken advantage of and nobody feels financially trapped.

Now, I know what some of you are thinking, because I thought it too: *Doesn't this create a weird power dynamic where the higher earner has more say in financial decisions?*

It can, if you let it. But that's a separate issue from the mechanics of contribution—that's about how you communicate and make decisions as a couple, which we'll dig into in Chapter 6. For now, just know this: contributing a higher percentage doesn't mean you get a louder voice. It means you're shouldering a proportional share of the collective load. The decision-making should still be collaborative, equal, and rooted in mutual respect.

The goal here isn't to create a hierarchy. It's to dismantle the hidden hierarchy that already exists when one person is financially stretched thin by an "equal" split while the other has money to burn.

Let me tell you what happened with Rachel and Matt, the couple I mentioned earlier. They switched to proportional contributions about two years ago. Rachel now covers 74% of their shared expenses (she got another raise; tech, you know), and Matt covers 26%. Their rent stayed the same, but Rachel contributes $1,370 and Matt contributes $480.

Here's what changed: Matt started saving. For the first time in their relationship, he had enough breathing room in his budget to put away $300/month toward an emergency fund. He stopped declining social invitations because he was broke. Rachel stopped feeling resentful that she couldn't suggest a nicer apartment or a long weekend away. They started talking about buying a house together—something that felt impossible when Matt was barely staying afloat.

The system didn't fix everything. They still argue about money sometimes (they're human). But the arguments are about actual disagreements—whether to prioritize paying off student loans or saving for a down payment—not about the unfairness baked into the foundation of how they split costs.

That's what proportional contribution does. It removes the structural unfairness so you can focus on the real decisions you need to make together.

One last technical note before we move on: revisit your percentages at least once a year. Life changes. People get raises, switch jobs, go back to school, take parental leave, launch side hustles. If your income shifts significantly—say, more than 10% up or down—recalculate your percentages and adjust your automatic transfers accordingly.

This isn't about nickels and dimes. It's about keeping the system aligned with your current reality so it continues to feel fair. A system that felt equitable two years ago might be quietly breeding resentment now if nobody's checked in on it.

Set a calendar reminder. First of the year, or your anniversary, or the start of summer—whatever anchor point you'll remember. Spend thirty minutes with a calculator, plug in your current take-home income, recalculate percentages, update your transfers. Then go get ice cream or something. Make it not a big deal.

Because here's the truth I wish I'd understood earlier: money systems in a relationship aren't one-time decisions you make and then forget about. They're living frameworks that need tending. The proportional contribution method isn't perfect—nothing is—but it's adaptable, transparent, and rooted in a principle that actually withstands real life.

It respects that you're two separate people with different earning capacities, different financial histories, and different goals. And it acknowledges that building a life together doesn't mean erasing those differences. It means creating a structure where both of you can contribute fairly, breathe freely, and move forward without one person silently drowning while the other wonders why things feel off.

That's the work. That's the whole point of the "Ours" account and proportional contributions: not to make everything perfectly equal, but to make the load proportionally bearable so you can both thrive.

But here's the question we haven't touched yet: what happens when an unexpected expense lands that doesn't fit neatly into your monthly budget?

Chapter 4: The 'Yours' Account Continued: Handling Unexpected Expenses

My friend Jessica called me at 11 PM on a Tuesday. Not unusual—we'd been friends since college, and late-night calls were part of our rhythm. What was unusual was that she was crying so hard I could barely understand her.

"He said I'm irresponsible," she finally managed. "All because my phone died."

It took me twenty minutes to piece together what had actually happened. Jessica's phone—the one she needed for work, for coordinating pickups with her kids' school, for everything—had stopped holding a charge. She'd taken it to the Apple store that afternoon. $89 for a battery replacement. She paid it without thinking twice, mentioned it to her husband Marcus that evening over dinner, and he'd exploded. Not because $89 was catastrophic. They could afford it. But because she "should have asked first" and because "these things always happen to you."

That last part was what broke her. The implication that needing a functioning phone was somehow a character flaw.

I'm telling you this because Jessica and Marcus had a budget. They split everything 50/50—rent, utilities, groceries, the works. They were textbook responsible. And they were slowly destroying their marriage over an $89 phone repair.

Here's what nobody tells you about budgeting as a couple: the shared expenses are the easy part. You can calculate mortgage payments and grocery bills in your sleep. It's the random stuff—the unreimbursed medical co-pay, the broken laptop, the car that decides to need new brakes on the same week your crown falls out—that reveals whether your system actually works or just looks good on paper.

Because here's what was really happening with Jessica and Marcus. They'd built a perfect system for predictable costs. But they had no mechanism for the unpredictable ones. So every time something broke or needed replacing, it triggered this awful calculus: Whose fault is this? Who should pay? Is this a "me" expense or an "us" expense? And beneath those questions lurked an even uglier one: Who's being more responsible?

I spent three years making this same mistake in my own marriage. We had our shared account, we had our personal spending money, we thought we'd covered all the bases. Then my transmission died. $2,100. I paid it out of savings without discussion because it felt like my car, my problem. My husband found out two weeks later when he was reconciling our accounts and asked why our emergency fund was suddenly $2,100 lighter. The fight that followed wasn't really about the money—we had it—but about the fact that I'd handled a major expense in complete isolation. He felt shut out. I felt judged. We were both right and both wrong, and our beautiful budget system had created the problem instead of solving it.

The cost of getting this wrong isn't financial. It's the slow accumulation of resentment. It's asking permission to fix things you need fixed. It's the mental load of constantly calculating whether your personal emergency qualifies as a household emergency. It's lying in bed at 2 AM doing math—if I pay for this myself, can I still afford the thing I was saving for? If I ask him to help cover it, will he think I'm bad with money?

And the really insidious part? This pattern makes you less likely to address small problems before they become catastrophic ones. You ignore the weird noise your car is making because taking it to the mechanic means having A Conversation. You put off the dentist because you're not sure if your cavity counts as a shared expense. The $200 fix becomes a $2,000 disaster, and now you're having that conversation anyway, except with much higher stakes and much worse options.

So let's talk about the 'Yours' account—not the fun money version for hobbies and lattes, but the version that actually protects your relationship from the stuff that will inevitably go wrong.

The expanded 'Yours' account is an emergency buffer that belongs to you individually. Not "ours." Not "ours but you manage your half." Yours. Money allocated to you, sitting in an account with only your name on it, designated specifically for the unexpected personal expenses that life throws at you.

I know what you're thinking. We just spent two chapters talking about shared responsibility and proportional contribution, and now I'm telling you to separate more money? Sounds contradictory. It's not. This is the piece that makes the whole system work.

Think about it this way. When your roof leaks, that's obviously a shared expense. You both live under that roof. When the refrigerator dies, shared expense—you're both eating that food. But when your work laptop crashes and needs a $700 repair? That's murkier. You need it for work, yes, but it's your job, your equipment. Or when you crack your phone screen—the phone you use for both work and personal stuff, the phone that's technically yours but functionally necessary for managing the household calendar and coordinating kids' pickups. Mine or ours?

The problem with trying to adjudicate these questions case-by-case is that you'll never agree on the right answer, and even when you do agree, the process of negotiating it every single time is exhausting. You're essentially relitigating the same argument with different props.

The 'Yours' emergency account solves this by creating a clear default: if it's your thing that broke, you pay for it from your account. Done. No negotiation required. No keeping score. No wondering if this particular emergency is important enough to bring to your partner.

But—and this is crucial—it only works if both of you are actually funding these accounts proportionally to your income and your exposure to unexpected costs. This isn't about fairness in some abstract sense. It's about acknowledging that life's random expenses don't distribute themselves equally.

Let me give you a real example. My cousin Lisa is a speech therapist who drives 200 miles a week visiting clients at different schools. Her husband Tom works from home as a software developer. In any given year, Lisa's car needs oil changes, tire rotations, occasional repairs, new wiper blades, maybe a battery. Tom's laptop might need a RAM upgrade or a new power cord. Guess whose unexpected expenses run higher?

They used to split everything 50/50, including car stuff, which seemed fair until you actually looked at usage. Tom drove Lisa's car maybe twice a month. Lisa used it forty hours a week for work. When it needed new brakes—$600—Tom agreed to split it, but he clearly felt like he was subsidizing her job. The resentment was subtle but real.

When they switched to the 'Yours' account system, they allocated more to Lisa's buffer specifically because her risk profile was higher. She put in $300 a month, he put in $150. Not because she made more—they earned almost the same—but because her circumstances meant she faced more frequent unpredictable costs. The brake job came out of her account. No discussion needed. No favors owed. And here's the thing that surprised them: Tom stopped mentally categorizing car repairs as "Lisa's problem that I generously helped with" and started thinking of them as just... handled. The cognitive shift was small but profound.

I still mess this up sometimes, by the way. Last year I had a root canal that insurance only partially covered—about $800 out of pocket. I paid it from my 'Yours' account without mentioning it to my husband until three weeks later, when it came up in conversation. He got quiet. Not angry exactly, but hurt. "I would have wanted to know," he said. And he was right. The system says I didn't need permission, but partnership means not treating the big stuff like classified information. So now our rule is: anything over $500, even if it's coming from individual accounts, gets at least a heads-up. Not asking for approval. Just keeping each other in the loop.

So how much should you actually put in these accounts?

I'm going to give you a framework, but I need you to understand something first: this isn't a prescription. This is a starting point that you'll adjust based on your actual life. The couples who get this right are the ones who track their spending for two or three months, look at what actually happened, and build their system around reality instead of aspirations.

Start with $500-$1,000 per person as a target balance. That's your cushion, sitting there ready for when things break. To get there, you'll likely need to allocate $150-$300 per month per person, depending on your risk profile and how quickly you want to build the buffer.

Risk profile matters more than income here. Ask yourself: - How old is your car? (Anything over 80,000 miles and you should be allocating more) - How's your health? (Chronic conditions that might need unexpected appointments or medications mean higher allocation) - What do you need for work? (Freelancers, people with equipment, anyone whose livelihood depends on specific tools or technology needs a bigger buffer) - How's your housing situation? (Renters have landlords to call when the water heater breaks; homeowners don't)

When Lisa and Tom were figuring out their allocations, Tom initially suggested they both put in the same amount—$200 a month each—because that "seemed fair." I walked them through the calculation. Lisa's car: 7 years old, 90,000 miles. Tom's car: he didn't have one. Lisa's health: generally good, but she had contacts (replacement lenses, solution, occasional eye appointments). Tom's health: fine, wore glasses he'd had for four years. Lisa's work equipment: needed reliable transportation, a decent phone for communicating with schools. Tom's work equipment: laptop that his company provided, personal computer he'd built himself and could repair.

Looking at it that way, Lisa's exposure to unexpected costs was clearly higher. So they landed on $300 for her, $150 for him, which gave them each about the same number of months to reach their target balance, but acknowledged that Lisa's target needed to be higher—$1,200 versus Tom's $600.

That felt unfair to Tom initially, until I pointed out that the alternative was continuing to split her car repairs 50/50 even though he barely used the car. "Which would you prefer?" I asked. "Putting an extra $150 into her account each month, or writing a check for $300 every time her car needs work?" He picked the first option immediately.

Here's where most couples screw this up: they set up the accounts, fund them for a few months, and then someone has an emergency, drains the account, and never refills it. Or both people go months without needing to tap their buffers, the money just sits there, and it starts to feel wasteful. Like, why are we parking $2,000 in these accounts when we could be paying down debt or investing?

This is the discipline part. The 'Yours' emergency accounts are insurance. You don't cancel your car insurance just because you haven't had an accident in six months. You don't let your balance drop to zero because you got lucky and nothing broke this quarter.

Treat the monthly allocation as non-negotiable. If Sarah's account dips to $200 because she had to replace her phone, next month she's putting in extra to build it back up to the target. If David's account sits at $1,000 for nine months straight, he doesn't reallocate that money to something else. It stays there, doing its job, which is being ready.

Now, if you both go a full year with no emergencies and your accounts are sitting above your target balance—like, you aimed for $1,000 and you're at $1,500—then yes, you can make a decision together about what to do with the excess. Redirect it to shared savings. Put it toward a vacation. Invest it. But the baseline stays intact.

The other thing that trips people up is the definition of "unexpected expense." Because if you're not careful, this turns into a loophole where everything becomes an emergency.

So let's be clear about what this account is for and what it's not for.

It IS for: - Repairs to things you personally own (car, phone, laptop, glasses) - Medical/dental costs not covered by insurance (co-pays, deductibles, prescriptions) - Work-related expenses that you can't get reimbursed for (professional development, certification renewals, replacing a work bag that wore out) - Replacing essential items that broke unexpectedly (winter coat, shoes you wear to work)

It's NOT for: - Upgrades you want but don't need (replacing a perfectly functional phone because a new model came out) - Hobbies and entertainment (that's what your fun money is for) - Gifts - Impulse purchases, even small ones - Bailing yourself out of bad planning (you forgot to budget for your annual car registration and now it's due)

The line between "need" and "want" gets fuzzy sometimes, I know. I struggle with this. Last fall I convinced myself I needed new running shoes because my old ones were "worn out," when really they just looked kind of dingy and I wanted an upgrade. I bought them with my emergency account money, then felt vaguely guilty about it for weeks. My husband didn't say anything—he couldn't have known whether my shoes were actually shot or not—but I knew I'd bent the rule.

Here's what I've learned: if you're questioning whether an expense qualifies, it probably doesn't. The true emergencies don't come with ambiguity. You know when your car won't start that it needs to be fixed. You know when the dentist shows you the X-ray of your cracked molar that it needs a crown. The things you have to talk yourself into? Those are wants dressed up as needs.

That said, you and your partner should define this together. Sit down and actually list out what counts as an emergency for your household. Lisa and Tom had a fascinating disagreement about this: Tom thought continuing education courses for Lisa's certification didn't count as emergencies because they were technically optional. Lisa pointed out that keeping her license active wasn't optional if she wanted to stay employed. They compromised: required CE credits came from the emergency fund, optional professional development came from her personal spending money.

Now let's talk about what happens when one person's expenses genuinely run higher than anticipated and they're constantly draining their account while the other person's sits full.

This happened with Jessica and Marcus, actually, after they finally set up this system. (Yes, the same Jessica from the beginning—she and Marcus did eventually figure it out, though it took couples therapy and about six months of very intentional practice.)

Jessica works in pharmaceutical sales, which means a lot of driving. Within four months of setting up their 'Yours' accounts, she'd had to use hers three times: new tires, a cracked windshield, and a laptop repair. Marcus, who worked in IT from home, hadn't touched his once. He started making comments. Not mean exactly, but pointed. “Must be nice to have an emergency fund that’s always there when you need it.” The implication being that Jessica was somehow causing these problems through negligence.

Here’s what their therapist helped them see: Jessica’s higher expenses weren’t a moral failing. They were a function of her job requirements. She drove 1,000 miles a month for work. Her employer reimbursed gas but not maintenance. Marcus worked from his spare bedroom and walked to the coffee shop when he needed a change of scenery. Their risk profiles were genuinely different.

So they adjusted. Jessica started putting in $400 a month instead of $250. Marcus dropped his to $100. This meant Jessica was allocating more of her income to emergency preparedness, but it also meant she stopped feeling like she was failing at budgeting every time something went wrong with her car.

The deeper issue was that Marcus had been unconsciously using money as a proxy for responsibility. Low expenses = responsible person. High expenses = careless person. Once he saw that in himself—once he really sat with how unfair that framework was—things shifted. Jessica’s windshield cracking from road debris wasn’t a character judgment. It was just bad luck, and the system they’d built was designed to absorb bad luck without creating conflict.

I think this is the piece that’s hardest for people who are used to 50/50 splits. Equal contribution feels like the only fair approach. But fairness isn’t about identical numbers. It’s about both people being equally protected and equally respected.

Here’s the practical setup, step by step, because I’ve seen people nod along with the concept and then get paralyzed trying to implement it.

Step One: Calculate your average monthly unpredictable expenses.

Go back through the last six months of bank and credit card statements. Pull out everything that wasn't a regular, planned expense. Car repairs, medical bills, broken appliances, replacing things that wore out. If you haven't been tracking expenses, estimate conservatively. Most people underestimate, so add 20% to whatever number you land on.

When my husband and I did this exercise, I genuinely thought my unexpected costs ran about $100 a month. Then I actually looked at the data. $350. Between pharmacy co-pays (I have a chronic condition that occasionally requires new prescriptions), occasional car stuff, and replacing things like my broken umbrella and the coffee maker that died, I'd been spending way more than I realized. That discrepancy explained a lot about why I always felt financially squeezed even though our budget looked fine on paper.

Step Two: Set your target balance and monthly contribution.

Your target balance should be enough to cover 3-4 months of those average unexpected expenses. If you calculated $200/month in unpredictable costs, aim for $600-$800 in your account.

Then figure out how fast you want to get there. Aggressive approach: fund it in 3 months by allocating the full amount. Conservative approach: build it over 6-12 months with smaller monthly allocations. There's no wrong answer, but be realistic about what you can actually sustain.

Step Three: Open a dedicated savings account.

Do not just mentally earmark money in your regular checking account. You need a separate account, ideally one that's easy to access (so you can transfer money when you need it) but not so easy that you accidentally spend it (so not connected to your debit card).

I use a high-yield savings account at an online bank. It takes about two business days to transfer money to my checking account, which is perfect—long enough that I won't impulse-spend it, short enough that I can access it when my car breaks down and I need to pay the mechanic.

Step Four: Define "unexpected personal expense" together.

Write it down. Literally make a list. This sounds ridiculously nitpicky, but it prevents so many arguments. When you're both stressed because something broke and you're trying to figure out how to pay for it, the last thing you want is to also be debating whether it qualifies for the emergency fund or should come out of somewhere else.

Lisa and Tom's list included: - Car repairs and maintenance (Lisa's car specifically; Tom didn't have one) - Medical/dental co-pays and deductibles - Replacing broken glasses or contacts - Work equipment repairs (Lisa's phone, Tom's laptop) - Replacing essential clothing that wore out (work shoes, winter coat)

Explicitly excluded: - Gifts for family or friends - Hobby-related purchases - Dining out - Vacation costs - Upgrading to new technology when current tech still worked

Step Five: Schedule regular check-ins.

Monthly or quarterly, sit down together and look at how the accounts are being used. This isn't about auditing each other. It's about noticing patterns. If one person is consistently draining their account and the other isn't, something needs to adjust—either the allocation amounts or the definition of what counts as an emergency.

Let me show you what this looks like in practice with one more couple: Aisha and James.

Aisha is a graphic designer, freelance. James is a middle school teacher. They earn roughly the same annual income—around $55,000 each—but Aisha's income fluctuates month to month while James's is steady. They've been married four years.

When they set up their 'Yours' accounts, they initially put in the same amount: $200 each per month. Within three months, Aisha had used hers twice (new laptop charger, dental cleaning that insurance only partially covered) and James hadn't touched his.

Then in month four, Aisha's computer crashed. Not totally dead, but limping along in a way that made her work harder and slower. A new laptop would cost $1,200. Her emergency account had $600 in it. She brought it to James.

"I need to replace my computer," she said. "I've got $600 saved, but it's going to cost more than that."

They looked at their options. Aisha could put the extra $600 on a credit card and pay it off over time. They could pull from their shared emergency fund. Or James could loan her money from his 'Yours' account, which had $800 sitting untouched.

Here's what they decided: Aisha would use her $600, they'd take $600 from the shared emergency fund (which they'd replenish over the next two months by each contributing an extra $150), and Aisha would increase her monthly allocation to her 'Yours' account to $300 going forward.

The computer wasn't really an unexpected expense in the emergency sense—Aisha knew she'd eventually need to replace it. But the timing was unexpected. She'd been planning to save up over the next year and buy a new one when she had the cash. The crash forced her hand.

What I love about how they handled this is that they didn't treat it as a failure of Aisha's planning. They treated it as new information about what her risk profile actually looked like. Freelancers need reliable equipment, and Aisha's work depended on her computer in a way that James's didn't. His school provided a laptop. If it broke, IT would replace it. Aisha's computer was both her most essential tool and her own responsibility.

Increasing her allocation to $300 a month meant she'd rebuild her emergency fund faster and be better prepared for the next time equipment failed. It wasn't punishment. It was adaptation.

One last thing I want to address, because it comes up every single time I talk about this system with couples: what if one person makes significantly more money than the other?

The principle stays the same. Allocations should be proportional to income. But the math gets a little more nuanced.

Let's say Partner A earns $80,000 and Partner B earns $40,000. That's a 2:1 ratio. If they've determined that their household needs $1,000 per month in individual emergency funds ($500 per person),

Partner A should be contributing roughly twice as much as Partner B to reach those targets. Maybe Partner A puts in $350/month and Partner B puts in $175/month, and they reach their respective $500 balances at the same rate.

But here's where it gets complicated: what if Partner A's risk profile is also higher? Maybe they drive more, have higher medical costs, own more equipment that could break. In that case, their target balance should probably be higher than $500. Maybe it should be $800. So now Partner A is putting in more money AND building to a higher target, while Partner B is putting in less money to reach a lower target.

This can feel deeply unfair if you're Partner A. You're already earning more (and presumably contributing more to shared expenses), and now you're also supposed to set aside more for your own emergencies?

Yeah. You are. Because the alternative is that when Partner A's expensive laptop breaks, or their car needs new tires, or they need a dental crown, that cost either comes out of shared funds (meaning Partner B is subsidizing expenses they didn't incur) or Partner A pays out of pocket and resents Partner B for not having to face the same costs.

The system works when both people are equally protected *relative to their circumstances*, not when both people contribute identical amounts.

I think one reason this is so hard for people is that we've internalized this idea that financial equality in a relationship means matching contributions dollar-for-dollar. It doesn't. It means both people have enough resources to handle their lives without constantly asking permission or feeling financially vulnerable.

When I had to replace my transmission for $2,100, I paid it myself because I felt like it was my car, my problem. But here's what I didn't see at the time: my husband and I were building a life together. We'd agreed that I'd take the job 45 minutes away because it paid better and had better benefits for both of us. That commute put wear on my car that wouldn't have happened if I'd taken the closer job with lower pay. The transmission wasn't just my problem. It was a consequence of a shared decision.

If we'd had the 'Yours' account system set up then, with proper allocations based on the fact that I was driving 500 miles a week, I would have had the money sitting there ready. No guilt. No weird financial math about whether I should ask him to help. No lying awake feeling like I'd made a unilateral decision that affected our joint finances.

The system would have handled it.

That's what you're building here. Not a rigid set of rules, but a structure that absorbs life's inevitable chaos without creating conflict. When something breaks—and something will always break—you want your first thought to be "how do we fix this," not "whose fault is this."

The 'Yours' emergency account is the piece that makes that possible. It says: you're an individual with your own needs and your own risks, and you deserve resources that are yours to deploy without negotiation. And also: we're building this together, so we're going to fund these accounts proportionally and fairly, based on what each of us actually faces.

That's not isolation. That's partnership. Real partnership, the kind that survives busted transmissions and cracked phone screens and all the other small disasters that make up a shared life.

So here's what you do next: Tonight, sit down with your partner. Pull out the last three months of statements. Start calculating. And then fund those accounts. Because something's going to break next week, or next month, and when it does, you'll already know exactly how you're going to handle it.

Chapter 5: The Conversation Starters: Spending Limits and Financial Secrets

My partner and I once had a screaming match over a $47 candle I bought without "permission." We weren't broke—we just had never discussed what counts as a joint decision versus a personal one. That candle sat on our shelf for months, a little wax monument to our lack of a system.

The fight wasn't really about the candle. It was about the fact that I'd spent nearly fifty dollars on scented wax without mentioning it, and my partner felt blindsided when they saw the charge. "You didn't even *ask* me," they said, which made me defensive because—why would I? It was my money. Except it wasn't, not entirely. We'd pooled our accounts six months earlier, and neither of us had bothered to define where "mine" ended and "ours" began.

That's the thing about spending limits. You don't realize you need them until you're standing in your living room at 9 PM, voices raised, arguing about bergamot and vanilla bean.

Most couples stumble into the same trap. They set up their Mine and Ours accounts, feel a brief surge of accomplishment, and assume the hard part is over. Then someone buys concert tickets. Or a new laptop. Or, in my case, an absurdly expensive candle. And suddenly you're not arguing about money—you're arguing about respect, autonomy, and whether your partner thinks you're fiscally responsible enough to be trusted with a debit card.

Here's what that pattern costs you: every undiscussed purchase becomes a potential landmine. You start second-guessing yourself before buying anything, which breeds resentment. Or you stop second-guessing entirely and just buy what you want, which breeds...

different resentment. Either way, you're eroding trust one transaction at a time. You think you're avoiding conflict by not talking about it, but you're actually *storing* conflict—tucking it away in your joint account statements, where it accumulates interest.

I've seen this play out dozens of times. Chris and Anya had their Mine and Ours accounts beautifully organized—proportional contributions, clear categories, the whole works. Then Chris bought a $250 noise-cancelling headset for work without mentioning it to Anya. When she saw the charge on their statement, she didn't explode. She just... deflated. That quiet disappointment is worse than anger, honestly. It's the feeling of being left out of your own financial life.

Chris thought he was in the clear because technically, the headset came from his share of their flexible spending. He'd justified it as a productivity investment—better audio on work calls, fewer distractions, that kind of thing. All true. But Anya didn't care about the justification. She cared that he'd made a significant purchase without looping her in, which made her feel like a roommate instead of a partner.

They worked it out over tea, which is apparently the universal beverage of financial reconciliation. Anya explained that it wasn't about controlling Chris's spending—she genuinely didn't care if he bought the headset. She just wanted to *know* about it. Chris admitted he'd avoided mentioning it because he was worried she'd think it was frivolous, which was its own problem (why are we partnering with people whose judgment we don't trust?). They landed on a simple threshold: anything over $100 required a heads-up. Not approval. Just awareness.

That distinction matters more than it sounds like it should. A "heads-up" system isn't about asking permission—it's about staying connected to your shared financial reality. Chris texts Anya: "Thinking about grabbing that headset we talked about, $250—sound good?" Anya sees the message, confirms she's aware, and Chris buys the headset. Thirty seconds of communication, zero lingering resentment.

(I still mess this up sometimes, by the way. Last month I bought a cookbook that was technically under our threshold, but I *knew* my partner would think it was unnecessary because we already own seventeen cookbooks. Did I mention it beforehand? No. Did I regret that when they raised an eyebrow at the package? Absolutely.)

But spending limits only solve half the problem. The other half—often the messier half—is financial secrets.

It's shockingly common for couples to hide purchases, downplay debt, or just... omit details about their financial lives. Not because they're malicious, but because money is tangled up with shame and fear in ways that are hard to articulate. You don't want your partner to think you're irresponsible. Or you're worried they'll judge you for a mistake you made years ago. Or you just want to maintain some illusion of control in a relationship where everything else feels joint and negotiated.

David and Sarah had a comfortable income—combined household around $120K, no kids, manageable rent. They weren't struggling. But Sarah discovered that David had been quietly accumulating credit card debt for several months, using it to fund small gifts for her. Flowers. Books she'd mentioned wanting. A nice dinner out. He thought he was being thoughtful, shielding her from the burden of those expenses.

When Sarah found the statements, she wasn't angry about the gifts. She was angry about the deception. David had been carrying around this secret, paying minimum balances, letting interest compound, all because he didn't want Sarah to feel like she had to contribute to her own surprises. Which is sweet in a deeply misguided way, but also incredibly damaging to the foundation of a partnership.

"I thought I was protecting you," David told her. Which is what everyone thinks when they keep financial secrets. You're protecting your partner from worry, or protecting yourself from judgment, or protecting some fragile sense of independence. But you're not protecting the relationship. You're corroding it.

The cost of financial secrets isn't just the money—though that's real enough. It's the trust you lose every day you keep the secret, and the trust you have to rebuild once it's out. Sarah didn't care about the debt itself. They could handle $3,000 in credit card charges. What she couldn't handle was the idea that David had been lying to her—actively, deliberately—for months. Every time she'd thanked him for flowers, he'd been hiding the fact that those flowers were purchased with debt he was keeping from her.

They started doing weekly "money dates," which sounds insufferably precious until you realize it's just a scheduled time to talk about finances without the weight of surprise or accusation. They'd sit down with their laptops, pull up their accounts, and go through everything together. Income, expenses, upcoming bills, any concerns. David agreed to a "no secrets" policy, which meant disclosing *all* of his accounts and debt, even the embarrassing stuff. Sarah did the same.

Here's what I learned from watching couples navigate this: you can't logic your way into financial honesty. You can't just *decide* to be transparent and expect that to override years of ingrained shame or fear. You have to build the scaffolding first—create an environment where vulnerability feels safe, where disclosure isn't met with anger or disappointment, where you both understand that past mistakes are just information, not indictments.

Sarah and David did a "financial vulnerability exercise," which is exactly as awkward as it sounds but also weirdly effective. They each wrote down three things they were hesitant to share about money. Past financial mistakes. Current anxieties. Spending habits they felt ashamed of. Then they read them aloud, taking turns, and the only rule was: listen without interrupting, and don't respond until your partner is completely finished.

David shared that he'd filed for bankruptcy in his early twenties after a failed business venture—something he'd never mentioned because he was embarrassed. Sarah shared that she still had $8,000 in student loan debt she'd been quietly paying off without telling him, because she didn't want him to think she was financially irresponsible. They both shared smaller anxieties too—David's tendency to overspend on takeout when he's stressed, Sarah's guilt about buying expensive skincare products.

None of it was catastrophic. But all of it mattered, because it was stuff they'd been carrying alone. Once it was out in the open, they could actually *deal* with it—make a plan for Sarah's student loans, set a takeout budget for David, acknowledge that skincare isn't frivolous if it makes Sarah feel good.

This took me three years to figure out, honestly. My partner and I went through our own version of this—less structured, more haphazard, involving at least one tearful conversation where I admitted I'd been secretly anxious about money since childhood and had no idea how to talk about it without feeling like I was failing. We didn't have a formal vulnerability exercise. We just... kept having the same fight about small purchases until we finally got tired of fighting and started talking about what was actually going on underneath.

What was going on underneath, for me, was a deep-seated belief that spending money on myself was selfish. What was going on for my partner was a fear that if we talked too openly about finances, it would turn into judgment and control. Neither of us was wrong, exactly. We were just operating from different scripts, written years before we met, and we'd never bothered to compare notes.

So we started comparing notes. We talked about how we were raised—my partner's family treated money as a private matter, something you didn't discuss even with your spouse, while my family talked about it constantly but in a way that was anxious and scarcity-focused. We talked about our worst financial fears—mine was ending up dependent on someone else, theirs was being seen as controlling or stingy. Once we understood where each other was coming from, it got easier to navigate the actual logistics of budgeting and spending limits.

But understanding doesn't happen in one conversation. It's a slow build. You have to keep showing up, keep being honest, keep resisting the urge to hide or deflect or minimize. And you have to create space for your partner to do the same.

Here's a practical framework that actually works, assuming you're both willing to engage honestly:

Start by picking one topic you've been avoiding. Maybe it's individual spending habits—those discretionary purchases that don't fit neatly into "bills" or "savings." Maybe it's past debt. Maybe it's just a general anxiety about whether you're both on the same page.

Whatever it is, name it explicitly. Don't dance around it.

Then schedule a time to talk about it. I know this sounds overly formal, but spontaneous financial conversations almost always go badly because someone feels ambushed. Pick a time when you're both calm, fed, and not rushed. Treat it like an important appointment, because it is.

When you sit down to talk, frame the conversation as collaborative information-gathering, not an interrogation. If you're trying to understand your partner's spending, don't ask "What did you spend your money on?"—that sounds accusatory. Try something like, "Could you walk me through a typical week of your spending? Just the things that aren't bills or our savings goals."

This is subtly different. It focuses on patterns, not isolated incidents. Your partner explains they usually grab coffee a couple times a week, maybe fifteen dollars total, and buy a book every weekend, around twenty dollars. Small amounts, but they add up.

Here's where most people go wrong: they immediately jump to judgment. "That's wasteful!" or "Do you really *need* coffee out?" Don't do that. Ask clarifying questions instead. "So those books—are you reading them cover-to-cover, or are they more of a casual enjoyment?" or "The coffee runs—is that something you look forward to as a little self-care during a busy day?"

You're not asking these questions to justify the expense. You're asking to understand the *why* behind it. Because once you understand why your partner is spending money on something, you can have a real conversation about whether it aligns with your shared values and goals.

Let's say your partner admits they've been buying new video games every month—small purchases, maybe fifty dollars total, but they don't even have time to play them. The temptation is to say, "See? You're wasting money on something you don't use!" But if you're actually trying to build understanding, you'd say something like, "That's interesting—it sounds like it's less about playing the games and more about the feeling of getting something new. Is that right?"

And maybe it is. Maybe your partner is trying to recapture a sense of excitement or control or novelty that's missing from other parts of their life. That's useful information. Now you can talk about whether there are better ways to meet that need, or whether fifty dollars a month is a reasonable price to pay for that feeling.

The same framework applies to financial secrets, except the stakes are higher and the defensiveness is stronger. If you discover your partner has undisclosed debt or a hidden account, your instinct is probably to feel betrayed and angry. Which is valid. But if you lead with "Why didn't you tell me about that?"—even if it's a fair question—you're almost guaranteed to trigger defensiveness.

Try this instead: "I was reviewing our finances and noticed an account I wasn't familiar with. Can you help me understand it?" You're asking for information, not placing blame. This gives your partner room to explain without feeling attacked.

If they reveal they've been carrying debt, resist the urge to immediately problem-solve or express disappointment. Just acknowledge their honesty first. "Thank you for telling me. I know that must have been difficult." Then, once the initial vulnerability has been honored, you can move into practical mode: "Let's figure out how to incorporate that into our overall plan."

I can't overstate how much easier this becomes when you've built a foundation of safety and trust. If your partner has previously felt judged or attacked when discussing money, they're going to be exponentially less likely to disclose difficult financial information. But if they know you'll approach the conversation with empathy and a genuine willingness to work together, they'll feel safer being vulnerable.

Mark and Lisa were trying to figure out why they kept arguing about money despite having similar incomes and relatively aligned goals. Mark is more frugal; Lisa enjoys occasional splurges on clothes and experiences. They'd been fighting about their different spending styles for months, each convinced the other was being unreasonable.

During their first real financial check-in, Mark started by saying, "Lisa, I've noticed we have different approaches to shopping. I sometimes feel anxious when you make larger purchases without discussing them first. It's not that I don't want you to enjoy things—I just want us on the same page."

That framing matters. He's not saying "You spend too much" or "You're irresponsible." He's describing his own emotional response and expressing a desire for connection. Lisa could hear that without getting defensive.

She responded, "Okay, that makes sense. Honestly, I often feel a little stifled when I have to justify every purchase. It feels like you're questioning my judgment."

Also fair. They're both naming their experiences without attacking each other.

Mark asked, "Can you tell me about your last big purchase? What prompted it and how did it make you feel?"

Lisa explained she'd bought a new dress for a friend's wedding, $150. She felt good wearing it—confident, put-together—but also guilty knowing Mark might disapprove.

Mark admitted he probably would have questioned it initially, not because he didn't want her to look nice, but because they were saving for a house down payment. Lisa said she understood their shared goal, but sometimes she just wanted to treat herself without feeling like she was derailing their entire financial future.

They compromised. A hundred dollars a month each as "fun money"—no questions asked, no justifications required. And any purchase over two hundred dollars would be discussed beforehand, not as a request for permission, but as an opportunity to make sure it fit within their overall plan.

This isn't revolutionary. It's just... communication. But it's communication with intention and structure, which is what most couples are missing. You're not trying to control each other's spending. You're trying to stay connected to your shared financial reality while honoring each other's autonomy.

The conversations won't always be easy. There will be moments of discomfort, disagreement, maybe even hurt feelings. That's normal. What matters is how you navigate those challenges. If things get heated, take a break. Agree to revisit the conversation later when you're both calmer. The goal isn't to win an argument—it's to find solutions that work for both of you.

Here's what I wish someone had told me earlier: financial transparency isn't a one-time achievement. It's an ongoing practice. You don't have one good conversation about money and then never have to think about it again. You have to keep showing up, keep being honest, keep adjusting your systems as your lives change.

My partner and I still have our spending threshold—anything over a hundred dollars gets mentioned before purchase—but we've adjusted it a few times over the years as our income has changed. When we were making less, a hundred dollars felt significant. Now it's less about the dollar amount and more about maintaining the habit of communication. Sometimes I text about a seventy-dollar purchase just because I know it's something my partner would want to be aware of. Sometimes they do the same.

And we still have our monthly money dates, though they're less formal now. We sit down with coffee (or wine, depending on the month), pull up our accounts, and just... talk. How are we feeling about our spending? Are there any upcoming expenses we need to plan for? Anything we're anxious about? It's not exciting. But it keeps us connected, and it prevents small financial tensions from building into major resentments.

The financial vulnerability exercises have become less structured too, but we still do them occasionally. If one of us is feeling anxious about money, or if we've made a mistake we're embarrassed about, we know we can bring it up without fear of judgment. That safety didn't exist by default. We had to build it deliberately, through consistent honesty and a lot of uncomfortable conversations.

David and Sarah—the couple dealing with his undisclosed credit card debt—took a similar approach. After their initial disclosure, they committed to weekly check-ins where they'd review all their accounts together. No secrets, no surprises. David agreed to be completely transparent about every card, every balance, every recurring charge. Sarah did the same.

They also set up a system where any new credit card or account had to be jointly discussed before opening. Not because they didn't trust each other, but because they'd learned that financial secrets—even small ones—create distance. They wanted to stay close.

It took about six months before those weekly check-ins started feeling natural instead of awkward. David said the first few were excruciating—he kept expecting Sarah to judge him or bring up past mistakes. But she didn't. She just listened, asked clarifying questions, and helped him think through strategies for paying down the debt faster.

Sarah admitted she struggled with her own impulse to control the situation. She wanted to take over David's finances entirely, make sure he wasn't making any more "mistakes." But she realized that wouldn't actually solve the problem—it would just shift the power dynamic in an unhealthy way. So she focused on being supportive instead of supervisory, which was harder than it sounds.

They paid off the credit card debt in about eighteen months. Not because they made massive sacrifices, but because they were finally working together instead of hiding from each other. And once the debt was gone, they kept doing the weekly check-ins anyway, because they'd realized the value wasn't just in tracking numbers—it was in maintaining connection and trust.

That's the thing about spending limits and financial secrets: they're not really about money. They're about the relationship underneath the money. You can have the most perfectly structured budget in the world, but if you're not communicating openly and honestly, it's not going to work. And you can have a messy, imperfect financial system, but if you're both committed to transparency and mutual respect, you'll probably be fine.

I don't believe in 50/50 splits, by the way—they're mathematically fair and emotionally bankrupt. Proportional contribution based on income is the only approach that respects both partners' autonomy and acknowledges that "equal" and "fair" aren't the same thing. But even proportional contribution doesn't mean anything if you're hiding purchases or keeping secrets about debt. The structure is just scaffolding. The real work is the ongoing practice of honesty.

So here's what I'd suggest: pick one conversation you've been avoiding. Maybe it's about spending habits. Maybe it's about past financial mistakes. Maybe it's just about whether you're both comfortable with how money is flowing through your relationship right now. Schedule a time to have that conversation—thirty minutes, an hour, whatever feels manageable. And then actually have it.

Start with curiosity, not accusation. Ask questions to understand, not to trap. Listen to hear, not to respond. Acknowledge your partner's honesty, especially if they're sharing something difficult. And remember that the goal isn't to solve every financial issue in one sitting—it's to build a foundation of trust and transparency that will make every future conversation easier.

If it helps, write down a few things you're hesitant to share about money before you start. Past mistakes. Current anxieties. Spending habits you feel weird about. Having them written down makes it easier to share them out loud without getting derailed or defensive. Your partner does the same. Then you take turns reading them, and the only rule is: listen without interrupting.

It will probably be uncomfortable. That's fine. Discomfort is just the feeling of growth happening. And the alternative—avoiding these conversations indefinitely—costs you far more than a few awkward moments. It costs you trust, connection, and the sense that you're actually building something together instead of just coexisting in the same financial space.

My partner and I still have that candle, by the way. We eventually laughed about the fight, but we also took it seriously enough to build a better system. Every time I smell bergamot now, I'm reminded that the smallest purchases can become the biggest conflicts if you're not paying attention. And that the real value of a spending limit isn't restriction—it's the freedom that comes from knowing you're both on the same page, working toward the same goals, without secrets between you.

That's what the next chapter is about, actually—what happens when "the same page" gets complicated by unequal incomes, and how power dynamics shift when one partner earns significantly more than the other. Because even with perfect transparency and thoughtful spending limits, money still carries weight. And that weight doesn't distribute evenly when the paychecks don't match.

Chapter 6: Unequal Earners: Navigating Power Dynamics

I once sat across from a client—let's call her Maria—who earned three times what her husband made, and she kept apologizing for "making things complicated."

She'd say it every few minutes. "I know it's complicated." "Sorry, this is probably making things harder." Her husband Carlos sat beside her, silent, arms crossed. He wasn't angry exactly. He looked resigned.

Maria was a pharmaceutical sales director pulling in $180,000 a year. Carlos taught middle school science and made $60,000. On paper, they were doing fine. They weren't fighting about money. They didn't have debt problems. But something was off, and Maria knew it, even if she couldn't name it yet.

What came out, slowly, over that first conversation, was that Maria had quietly taken over *everything* financial. She paid all the bills. She managed their investments. She made decisions about their retirement accounts, their insurance, their savings goals. When I asked Carlos if he knew how much they had in savings, he shrugged. "Maria handles it." When I asked Maria why, she said, "I just thought... it seemed easier. He's so busy with work and grading papers. I didn't want to burden him."

But that wasn't the whole truth, and she knew it. Her guilt about out-earning him had quietly turned into financial control. She was managing everything "to make it easier on him," but really she was protecting herself from his resentment. Or maybe from her own fear that he resented her. Either way, they'd created a dynamic where Carlos had been slowly, incrementally pushed out of financial decision-making in his own marriage.

He didn't feel like a partner. He felt like a dependent.

And that's the thing about income disparities in relationships. The problem isn't the money. It's what the money *represents*. It's the power dynamics that develop, often invisibly, when one person brings in significantly more than the other. Those dynamics don't announce themselves. They don't show up as obvious fights. They show up as patterns. One person starts "handling" things. The other person starts deferring. Before long, you've got a relationship where financial decisions—and sometimes all major decisions—flow in one direction.

I don't believe in 50/50 splits. I think they're mathematically fair and emotionally bankrupt. Equal and fair aren't the same thing, and pretending they are causes more problems than it solves.

Think about it. If one partner makes $150,000 and the other makes $50,000, splitting expenses down the middle means the lower earner is contributing a vastly larger percentage of their income. They're squeezed tight while their partner has breathing room. That's not fair. That's lazy math dressed up as equality.

But the alternative—where the higher earner just covers everything—creates its own disaster. The lower earner loses autonomy. They start asking permission to spend money. They feel like a child asking their parent for an allowance. And the higher earner, no matter how generous they are, starts to feel like they're carrying the whole load. Resentment builds on both sides.

Proportional contribution is the only approach that respects both partners' autonomy and acknowledges reality. You earn more, you contribute more. Not because you're superior, but because you *can*. And the lower earner still contributes meaningfully, maintaining dignity and partnership.

Here's how it works in practice.

Sarah and Ben were stuck in the 50/50 trap. Sarah was a surgeon making $220,000. Ben was a freelance graphic designer pulling in maybe $75,000 in a good year. They'd started their relationship splitting everything evenly because it "seemed fair." But Ben was constantly stretched. His half of the rent felt like a weight. His half of the utilities, the groceries, the car insurance—it all added up. He was living paycheck to paycheck while Sarah had money left over every month.

Sarah, meanwhile, was frustrated. She didn't understand why Ben would occasionally drop $300 on a new drawing tablet or $150 on art supplies when he was supposedly "broke." To her, it looked irresponsible. To Ben, it was his work. Those tools weren't luxuries; they were how he made a living. But he felt guilty defending the purchases because he knew Sarah was carrying more of the emotional weight of their finances, even though their contributions were technically equal.

They weren't fighting openly. But there was this tension. This chill.

What they needed—and what they eventually figured out—was a system that acknowledged Sarah's higher income without erasing Ben's contribution. They shifted to proportional contributions based on income percentage.

Here's the math. Sarah earned roughly 75% of their combined income. Ben earned 25%. Their essential monthly expenses—rent, utilities, groceries, insurance, car payments—totaled $5,000. Instead of splitting that $5,000 down the middle ($2,500 each), Sarah contributed 75% ($3,750) and Ben contributed 25% ($1,250).

Sarah's remaining income after her contribution: $14,583 per month. Ben's remaining income after his contribution: $5,000 per month.

See the difference? Both partners were now contributing proportionally, which meant both had disposable income left over relative to what they earned. Ben wasn't drowning. Sarah wasn't resentful. And critically, Ben could buy his art supplies without feeling like he was stealing from their shared financial health, because that money was *his*—money he'd earned and had left over after contributing his fair share.

This isn't about punishing the higher earner. It's about creating a system where both people can breathe.

But the conversation around proportional contribution needs to go deeper than just paycheck math. Because in a lot of relationships—especially those with kids, or where one partner has scaled back their career, or where someone's doing the invisible labor that keeps a household running—income is only part of the picture.

Let me tell you about Jenna and Marcus. Jenna had been a marketing director before their first kid was born. She'd been making $95,000. Marcus was an engineer making $130,000. When their daughter arrived, they ran the numbers and realized daycare would cost nearly $2,000 a month. Jenna's commute was brutal—90 minutes each way. Marcus's job had more flexibility. They decided Jenna would go part-time, working three days a week from home and taking a pay cut down to $50,000.

On paper, it looked like Marcus was now the primary earner. And he was. But here's what the paycheck didn't show: Jenna was now doing the majority of the childcare, the meal planning, the grocery shopping, the laundry, the doctor's appointments, the school pickups, the emotional labor of remembering every birthday and organizing every family gathering. She was working her three professional days, sure. But the other four days? She was working just as hard. She just wasn't getting paid for it.

Marcus didn't see it that way at first. He started thinking of his income as "their" income in a way that subtly shifted the power dynamic. He'd make comments like, "Well, I'm paying for most of this, so..." Not in a cruel way. Just... stating facts. But those facts felt like tiny cuts to Jenna. She was working her ass off. She just wasn't being compensated.

This is where the "contribution inventory" comes in, and it's one of the most eye-opening exercises couples can do. It's tedious, yes. But it's worth it.

Here's how it works. For one full week, both partners track *everything* they do. Not just paid work. Everything. Break it down into specific tasks with time estimates.

Jenna's week looked like this: - Professional work (marketing): 24 hours - Childcare: 35 hours - Meal planning and cooking: 8 hours - Grocery shopping: 3 hours - Laundry and household cleaning: 6 hours - Organizing family logistics (appointments, school forms, etc.): 4 hours

Total: 80 hours of work per week.

Marcus's week: - Professional work (engineering): 45 hours - Childcare (evenings and weekends): 10 hours - Yard work and home maintenance: 3 hours - Cooking (weekend breakfasts): 2 hours

Total: 60 hours of work per week.

When they sat down and actually *looked* at those numbers, Marcus was stunned. He'd genuinely thought he was carrying the heavier load because his paycheck was bigger. But Jenna was working 20 more hours per week than he was, doing labor that was just as essential to their household functioning. If they'd had to pay someone to do her childcare, meal prep, and household management, it would've easily cost $50,000 a year or more.

So what do you do with that information?

Some couples assign an estimated hourly rate to household tasks—$20/hour for childcare, $25/hour for cooking, $30/hour for cleaning—and calculate "contribution points." It's not about creating a rigid ledger. It's about making visible the work that usually stays invisible.

For Jenna and Marcus, the exercise shifted how they thought about money. They stopped thinking of Marcus's income as "his" or even as "theirs" in a way that centered his earning. They started thinking of their household as a joint enterprise where both of them were contributing essential labor. Jenna's unpaid work had real value. And their budget needed to reflect that.

They restructured their finances so Jenna had independent control over a "household operations" budget of $2,000 per month—covering groceries, kids' activities, household supplies, and her personal spending money. It wasn't an allowance Marcus was giving her. It was compensation for work she was doing that benefited both of them. And all major financial decisions—investments, big purchases, savings goals—were made together, as equals, regardless of who was bringing in the bigger paycheck.

This is the shift that has to happen when incomes are unequal. You have to expand your definition of "contribution" beyond salary. Otherwise, you're building a financial system on a foundation that ignores half the work being done.

But even when you've acknowledged the full scope of contributions, there's still the question of power. Because money and power are tangled up in ways that are hard to untangle. The person who earns more often, subtly, ends up with more say. They don't necessarily intend to. It just happens.

I see this all the time, and honestly, I still mess this up sometimes. I'll be explaining a budgeting principle to a couple and realize mid-sentence that I'm unconsciously directing my advice more toward the higher earner, as if they're the "real" decision-maker. It's a reflex. Our culture trains us to equate income with authority. Breaking that reflex takes deliberate effort.

Here's what that effort looks like in practice.

First, you need shared decision-making structures that prevent one person from dominating. It's not enough to just say, "We'll talk about big purchases." You need a framework.

Try this: establish spending tiers with different approval processes.

Tier 1: Automatic expenses. Rent, utilities, insurance, minimum debt payments. Both partners have full visibility into these. They're non-negotiable, and they happen every month without discussion.

Tier 2: Regular predictable expenses. Groceries, gas, household supplies, kids' activities. Each partner gets a pre-approved spending limit they can manage independently. No asking permission. If you're under the limit, you're good.

Tier 3: Discretionary personal spending. Each partner gets an agreed-upon amount they can spend however they want, no questions asked. This is sacred. You don't get to interrogate your partner about whether they "really need" that thing. If it's within their personal spending budget, it's their call.

Tier 4: Large purchases and financial goals. Anything over a certain threshold—say, $500—requires a conversation. Not just "Can we afford this?" but "How does this fit with our priorities? What are we trading off?"

That last tier is where real partnership happens. And it requires structure, because without it, the higher earner's voice tends to dominate.

David and Rachel had this problem. David was a software engineer making $160,000. Rachel was a social worker making $52,000. David wasn't trying to be controlling, but he'd fallen into the habit of making unilateral decisions about their investments. He'd research index funds, rebalance their portfolio, open new retirement accounts—all without consulting Rachel. In his mind, he was "handling it" so she didn't have to worry. In Rachel's mind, she was being excluded from decisions about *their* money.

When they finally talked about it—really talked, not just Rachel dropping hints and David not picking them up—Rachel said something that landed: "I don't need you to protect me from financial decisions. I need you to include me in them."

So they created a rule. Any financial decision over $500, or any change to their investment strategy, required a joint meeting. They'd both do research beforehand. They'd each come with their perspective. And they'd make the decision together. Sometimes that meant David explaining investment concepts Rachel wasn't familiar with. Sometimes it meant Rachel pointing out priorities David hadn't considered. The point wasn't that every decision required perfect consensus. The point was that both voices were heard.

Here's another thing they did that helped: they scheduled monthly "money dates." Not crisis meetings when something went wrong. Regular, proactive check-ins. They'd go over their spending for the month, look at progress toward their goals, and talk about anything that felt off. Those conversations became a space where Rachel could say, "Hey, I noticed you moved money into a new fund without mentioning it," and David could say, "You're right, I should've brought that up first." The regularity of the check-ins meant small issues got addressed before they became big resentments.

These structures matter because they counteract the gravitational pull of income-based power dynamics. Without them, it's too easy for the higher earner to drift into the driver's seat. With them, you're building equality into the system itself.

Let me give you one more example, because I think this is where a lot of couples get stuck.

Nina and Greg. Nina's a dentist making $210,000. Greg's a high school English teacher making $58,000. They'd been together for eight years, married for five. Early on, they'd tried a proportional contribution system and it worked okay. But over time, Nina started feeling like she was subsidizing Greg's life. He'd take summers off—teachers do—and she'd be working through August while he was, in her words, "relaxing." She didn't say this out loud, not directly. But it came out in little jabs. "Must be nice to have the summer off." "I wish I could take three months to read books."

Greg felt it. He started feeling defensive about his job, about his income, about his entire career. He loved teaching. But Nina's comments made him feel like he'd chosen wrong, like he should've prioritized money over meaning.

When they came in to talk, the resentment was thick. Nina felt like she was carrying them financially. Greg felt like his work—shaping kids' lives, for god's sake—wasn't valued.

Here's what they were missing: they'd never actually aligned on their values around work and money. Nina valued financial security and independence. Greg valued meaningful work and work-life balance. Neither was wrong. But they'd never explicitly said, "Okay, here's what matters to each of us. How do we build a financial system that honors both?"

Once they named it, things shifted. They agreed that Greg's teaching career was a shared choice they were both making, not something Nina was "putting up with." That meant his summers off weren't a luxury he was enjoying while she worked—they were part of a lifestyle they'd chosen together. They restructured their budget to reflect that. Nina contributed more to their joint expenses, yes, because she earned more. But Greg's contribution—both financial and in terms of household labor—was valued explicitly. And they made a rule: no jabs. If Nina was feeling resentful about carrying more of the financial weight, she had to say it directly, not let it leak out in passive-aggressive comments.

It took time. But the shift was real. They stopped keeping score. They started thinking of their finances as a joint project where both of them were bringing different but equally important resources.

That's the mindset shift that has to happen when incomes are unequal. You're not splitting things. You're building something together. And that means recognizing all the ways each person contributes, assigning value to work that doesn't come with a paycheck, and creating decision-making structures that prevent income from translating directly into power.

So here's where you start.

Tonight, or this weekend—whenever you can carve out an hour—sit down with your partner and do the contribution inventory. Track everything you both do over the next week. Be specific. Don't just write "housework." Write "laundry, 2.5 hours" and "meal prep, 6 hours" and "kid's school project, 1 hour." At the end of the week, compare notes. Look at the total hours each of you is working, paid and unpaid.

Then have the conversation. Not about blame. About fairness. About building a system where both of you feel valued. Ask each other: Does our current budget reflect the reality of our contributions? If one of us is working significantly more unpaid hours, how do we account for that? If there's an income disparity, are we splitting expenses proportionally or equally, and does that feel fair to both of us?

And here's the thing about fairness—it's not a static target. What feels fair today might not feel fair in six months. One of you might get a raise. Or lose a job. Or take on more childcare. Or go back to school. Life changes. Your financial system has to be flexible enough to change with it.

Which is why the monthly check-in isn't optional. It's not something you do when things are broken. It's the maintenance that keeps things from breaking in the first place.

Chapter 7: Tracking and Reviewing: The Monthly Financial Check-In

Sarah checked her bank account on a Tuesday afternoon in March and felt her stomach drop. The balance was $347 lower than she'd expected. She stared at the screen, trying to piece together where it had gone—groceries, sure, and that thing she'd ordered online last week, but what else? She couldn't remember. Worse, she had no idea what Ben had spent from their joint account, and asking felt like accusing. So she didn't ask. She just felt a low-grade anxiety settle in her chest and stayed there for the rest of the week.

That's the hidden cost of not tracking your money together. It's not dramatic. There's no shouting match, no bounced check (not yet, anyway). It's just this quiet, creeping unease—the sense that you're not quite in control, that something could go wrong and you wouldn't see it coming. You might overspend without realizing it. Or your partner might. And by the time either of you notices, you're already behind, already defensive, already primed for conflict. The stakes feel higher because they *are* higher—you've lost the chance to course-correct early, when it's easy.

I learned this the hard way. My partner and I went nearly six months once without doing any kind of formal review. We weren't being reckless—we paid our bills on time, we weren't in debt—but we also had no idea if we were making progress toward anything. Our savings account grew, but slowly, and we couldn't tell you why some months were better than others. When we finally sat down to look at the numbers, we discovered we'd been hemorrhaging money on subscription services we'd forgotten about. Seventy-three dollars a month, gone, for things we didn't use. That's nearly $900 a year. We could've taken a weekend trip. We could've put it toward the down payment we kept saying we were saving for. Instead, it just… leaked away.

So here's what I wish someone had told us back then: tracking your money isn't about control or restriction. It's about *seeing* what's actually happening, so you can make real decisions instead of just reacting to whatever your bank balance happens to be that day.

A monthly financial check-in is the single most effective tool for preventing that slow financial drift. It's a standing appointment where you and your partner sit down, look at the money together, and ask a few simple questions: Where did it go? Where do we want it to go next? Are we still on the same page? That's it. You're not auditing each other. You're not rehashing every purchase. You're just making sure you both know what's happening with the money you share.

Most couples resist this. They'll tell you they don't have time, or that it feels too formal, or that they're already communicating fine. But what they mean is: talking about money feels uncomfortable, and we'd rather avoid it. Which is fair. Money conversations *can* be uncomfortable, especially if you've had bad ones before. But avoidance doesn't make the discomfort go away—it just delays it until the stakes are higher and the emotions are sharper. A scheduled check-in, on the other hand, makes the conversation routine. Predictable. Low-stakes. You're catching small issues before they become big ones.

The first step is stupidly simple: put it on the calendar. Seriously. Treat it like a doctor's appointment or a dinner reservation. Pick a day that works for both of you—first Sunday of the month, last Saturday, whatever—and block out thirty to sixty minutes. If you don't schedule it, it won't happen. Life will fill that space with something else, and three months will go by before you realize you haven't talked about money once.

And here's the thing: it doesn't have to be long. Half an hour is usually enough, especially once you've done it a few times and gotten into a rhythm. You're not doing your taxes here. You're just checking in. The goal is consistency, not perfection.

Where you do this matters more than you'd think. Don't try to have this conversation while one of you is cooking dinner or while the TV's on in the background. Sit down somewhere comfortable, away from distractions. Turn your phones on silent. This isn't about being overly formal—it's about signaling to each other that this matters, that you're both here, paying attention.

Now: what do you actually *talk about* during these thirty to sixty minutes?

Start with wins. I mean it. Before you look at a single number, take five minutes to talk about what went *right* last month. Did you stick to your grocery budget? Did one of you find a great deal on car insurance? Did you resist an impulse purchase you would've made six months ago? Celebrate it. Out loud. This isn't touchy-feely nonsense—positive reinforcement is how you build momentum. If every money conversation starts with criticism or problem-solving, you'll start dreading them. But if you kick things off by acknowledging progress, even small progress, the whole tone shifts. You're on the same team, and the team is winning.

After that, move into the spending review. This is where you compare what you *planned* to spend with what you *actually* spent, category by category. Pull up your tracking app, your spreadsheet, your notebook—whatever system you're using—and go through it together. Groceries. Transportation. Utilities. Entertainment.

Here's the key: you're not looking for someone to blame. You're looking for patterns. If you budgeted $600 for groceries and spent $750, the question isn't "Who overspent?" It's "What happened?" Maybe you had people over for dinner twice. Maybe prices went up. Maybe you got sick and ordered takeout more than usual. All of those are useful pieces of information. They tell you whether you need to adjust your budget, change your habits, or just roll with it because it was a one-off.

I'll be honest—this part still trips me up sometimes. My instinct, when I see we've gone over budget somewhere, is to get a little defensive, like I need to justify every purchase. It took me a couple years to realize my partner wasn't interrogating me. We were just looking at the facts. Once I stopped treating it like a performance review and started treating it like a collaborative puzzle—"Huh, interesting, let's figure out what happened here"—the whole thing got easier.

Let's say you budgeted $400 for dining out and you spent $620. You look at the transactions and realize that most of it came from one weekend when friends were visiting. Okay. So was that worth it? If the answer is yes, great—you made a conscious trade-off, and you'll adjust somewhere else or just accept that this month was higher. If the answer is no, if it felt more stressful than fun, then you've learned something useful: maybe next time you host, you cook at home instead of going to restaurants. Either way, you're *learning*. You're getting smarter about how you want to spend.

Next, check in on your bigger goals. This is the part that keeps you from getting tunnel vision. It's easy to focus only on the day-to-day expenses and lose sight of why you're doing any of this in the first place. So take ten minutes to ask: How are we doing on the things that matter? Are we on track to pay off that credit card? Are we building our emergency fund at the pace we wanted? Are we saving enough for the vacation we talked about?

If the answer is no, don't panic. Just ask: what needs to change? Do we need to cut back somewhere? Do we need to increase our income? Do we need to adjust the timeline on this goal because life happened and that's okay? The point isn't to shame yourselves for falling short. The point is to make sure you're still moving in the direction you want to go.

This is also when you talk about upcoming expenses. Not just bills—those are predictable—but the stuff that's easy to forget until it's suddenly urgent. Is someone's birthday coming up? Do you need to book flights for a wedding? Is your car registration due? Is it time to replace the tires you've been putting off? Getting these things on your radar *now* means they don't blindside you later. Keep a running list somewhere—a shared note on your phone, a section in your budgeting app—and add to it as you think of things. Then, during your check-in, go through that list together and figure out how you'll handle each item.

Here's where I've seen a lot of couples get stuck: they do the check-in, they identify the problems, and then... nothing changes. They just have the same conversation next month. That's because they're missing the final step, which is the forward look. Before you close out the meeting, spend five or ten minutes talking about next month. What are your priorities? Are there any changes you need to make to the budget? Any opportunities to save a little more or reallocate funds?

This is also your chance to adjust categories that aren't working. Maybe you've been consistently overspending on groceries because your initial estimate was unrealistic. Fine—bump it up, and cut back somewhere else that has room to give. Or maybe you realize you've been underutilizing a category—you budgeted $200 for hobbies but only spent $60. Great. You can reallocate that surplus toward a goal that matters more right now. Your budget is a living document. It should change as your life changes.

Let me walk you through what this looked like for Ben and Maria, a couple I know who started doing monthly check-ins about a year ago. They'd been together for three years, living together for one, and they'd never really talked about money beyond "Can you Venmo me for half the rent?" When they sat down for their first check-in, it was awkward. They didn't know what to say. They pulled up their bank accounts and just kind of stared at the numbers.

But they stuck with it. The second month was a little easier. By the third month, they had a rhythm. They'd discovered that Maria was spending about $150 a month on books—not a problem, but something she hadn't realized. Ben was spending close to $200 on lunches out, which *was* a problem, because he'd been complaining about not having enough left over to save. Once they could see the pattern, they could talk about it. Ben started packing lunch three days a week. That freed up about $90 a month, which they started putting toward an emergency fund.

The breakthrough moment came in month five. They looked at their progress and realized they'd saved $1,100 in their emergency fund without it feeling painful. That was more than they'd saved in the entire previous year. They weren't making more money. They weren't depriving themselves. They were just *aware* of where their money was going, and that awareness let them make better choices.

Now, the monthly check-in only works if you're actually tracking your spending *between* check-ins. You can't show up once a month, look at your bank balance, shrug, and call it good. You need data. Real data. That means recording your expenses—ideally every few days, at minimum once a week—so you know where your money is going *while* it's happening, not after the fact.

I know. I know. This is the part where people's eyes glaze over. They imagine spreadsheets with thousands of rows, or spending hours every night entering receipts. But it doesn't have to be that complicated. A simple spreadsheet works. Four columns: date, category, amount, who spent it. That's it. Or use an app if that's easier—Mint, YNAB, even just the notes app on your phone. The tool doesn't matter. What matters is that you use it, and that you both have access to the same information.

Some couples split this up: one person tracks groceries and household stuff, the other tracks transportation and utilities. Others do it individually and then combine everything during the check-in. There's no right way. The key is transparency. You both need to be able to see where the money's going, so there are no surprises and no secrets.

Tracking also shifts the frame from blame to curiosity. If you wait until the end of the month to discover you overspent, it's easy to point fingers. But if you're checking in weekly, you catch it early. You see the pattern forming—"Huh, we've already spent $400 on groceries and it's only the 15th"—and you can adjust. Maybe you skip the fancy cheese this week. Maybe you eat out one less time. Small corrections, made early, keep you on track without requiring heroic willpower or dramatic sacrifices.

Let's say you're tracking your spending and you notice you spent $80 on coffee last month. That might feel insignificant day-to-day—it's just a latte, it's four bucks, who cares? But $80 a month is $960 a year. That's a plane ticket. That's a new laptop. That's a meaningful chunk of your emergency fund. I'm not saying you have to cut out coffee—I haven't, I probably never will—but at least now you're *choosing* it. You know what it costs, and you've decided it's worth it. That's different from just drifting through your days, swiping your card, and wondering where the money went.

Here's a framework you can use for daily or weekly tracking: divide your spending into three buckets—Needs, Wants, and Savings. Every time you spend money, ask yourself which category it belongs in. Groceries? Need. Movie tickets? Want. Transfer to your emergency fund? Savings. At the end of the week, add up each category. This won't give you a granular view of every transaction, but it will show you the big picture: are you spending more on wants than you realized? Are you actually saving as much as you thought?

David and Emily tried this for a month. They were trying to save for a down payment on a house, but they kept falling short of their goal. When they tracked their spending using the Needs/Wants/Savings framework, they discovered they were spending about $300 a month on wants they didn't even value that much—subscription services they'd forgotten about, impulse purchases that sat unused, delivery fees that added up faster than they'd realized. They didn't cut out *all* of it—some of those wants brought them real joy—but they trimmed about $180 a month and redirected it to savings. That one change got them back on track.

But tracking isn't only about cutting back. It's also about recognizing what's working. Did you stay within your grocery budget this month? That's a win. Did you negotiate a lower rate on your internet bill? That's a win. Did you resist buying something you wanted but didn't need, and a week later you'd forgotten about it entirely? *That's a win.* Celebrate those moments. They're evidence that you're building new habits, that the system is working.

You might be thinking: this sounds like a lot of work. And yeah, it is work. But so is fighting about money. So is the anxiety of not knowing if you can afford something. So is realizing six months from now that you're no closer to your goals than you were today. Tracking and reviewing takes time, but it saves you from spending *more* time cleaning up the mess that comes from not doing it.

One thing I'll tell you: don't be rigid about this. Life changes. Jobs change. Kids happen. Emergencies happen. Your budget needs to bend with that. If you set up a beautiful system in January and then stubbornly stick to it even though your circumstances shifted in March, you're setting yourself up for frustration. The budget is a tool. Tools are supposed to make your life easier, not harder. If something isn't working, change it.

After a few months of consistent check-ins, you'll start to notice something interesting: the conversations get shorter. Not because you're skipping steps, but because you've built shared understanding. You both know where the money is, where it's going, what the priorities are. The check-in becomes less about discovery and more about maintenance. You're just making sure nothing's slipped, adjusting as needed, and moving on.

That's when the real value shows up. It's not just that you're hitting your savings goals or staying out of debt—though those are great. It's that you've removed a massive source of stress from your relationship. Money stops being this vague, anxious thing you avoid talking about. It becomes a regular, manageable part of your life together. You trust each other more, because you're not guessing or assuming—you *know*. And that trust carries over into everything else.

So here's what I want you to do: pick a date. Right now. First Sunday of next month, last Saturday, whatever works. Put it on your calendar. Thirty minutes. Label it "Financial Check-In" or "Money Date" or whatever makes you both actually show up. Then, before that date, start tracking your spending. It doesn't have to be perfect. Just write down what you spend for the next two weeks. When the check-in comes, bring that information with you, sit down together, and go through it. Start with wins. Then review the spending. Then talk about your goals. Then look ahead to next month.

That's it. You don't need a fancy system. You don't need an advanced degree in finance. You just need to show up, look at the numbers together, and talk about what you see. The first time will feel awkward. The second time will feel a little easier. By the third or fourth time, it'll start to feel normal. And six months from now, when you realize you've saved more, fought less, and actually made progress on the things you said mattered—you'll wonder why you didn't start sooner.

But only if you start. Only if you decide that this month, this week, *today*, you're going to stop drifting and start steering. And the next chapter? That's where we'll talk about what to do with that momentum once you've built it—how to take those shared goals you've been naming in your check-ins and turn them into something real.

Chapter 8: Long-Term Goals & The 'Ours' Account

They were sitting in their financial advisor's office when the truth came out. Ten years married, and Sarah discovered that while she'd been meticulously funneling money into a college fund for their two kids—sacrificing weekend getaways, new clothes, even the occasional dinner out—Mark had been stockpiling cash in a separate account for what he called his "exit fund." Not from the marriage, he insisted. From his job. He wanted to retire early. Travel. Maybe buy a boat.

The advisor, to her credit, kept a straight face. Sarah didn't.

"You've been saving for a *boat*," she said, "while I've been skipping Target runs to save for tuition?"

Mark looked genuinely baffled. "We never talked about it being one or the other."

And that's the thing—they hadn't talked about it at all.

This is the conversation most couples avoid until they're sitting across from each other in some professional's office, or worse, lying awake at three in the morning realizing they've spent a decade pulling in opposite directions. One partner's dreaming of early retirement while the other's calculating compound interest on a future grandchild's college fund. One's budgeting for a house in the suburbs; the other's researching extended backpacking trips through South America.

These aren't conflicts, exactly. They're just different pictures of the future that nobody thought to compare.

And here's what that costs you: it's not dramatic. You don't wake up one day and find your marriage in ruins because you disagreed about retirement timelines. The cost is quieter. It's the slow accumulation of resentment when you skip the vacation you wanted because your partner's focused on paying down the mortgage faster, and you never actually agreed that was the priority. It's the growing sense that you're building something alone, even though you're supposedly doing this together.

It's looking up one day and realizing you've been married for fifteen years and you still don't know what you're working *toward* as a couple—just what you're working *against*: debt, bills, the vague specter of an insecure future.

I did this for three years. My partner wanted to save aggressively for a down payment on a house. I was more focused on keeping our student loans from ballooning and maybe—*maybe*—taking a real vacation once in a while instead of visiting family for the fourth year running. We never fought about it, which somehow made it worse. We just quietly pursued our separate financial agendas, each assuming the other was on board, until one night she asked why I hadn't been contributing more to the house fund and I realized I'd been treating it like *her* goal, not *ours*.

She'd been doing the same with my loan repayment strategy. We were roommates with joint checking, not partners with a shared vision.

Those three years didn't just cost us money—though they did. We'd have reached the down payment faster if we'd been coordinated. The loans would've shrunk quicker. But the real cost was the distance that opened up between us. Little comments that landed wrong. The time she came home excited about an open house she'd toured and I barely looked up from my laptop because I was comparing refinancing options for my loans. The weekend I suggested we splurge on a beach trip and she got this pinched look on her face, and I knew she was mentally calculating how much closer to the house that money would've gotten her.

We were living in the same apartment, sleeping in the same bed, and building completely separate futures.

So before we talk about *how* to save for long-term goals, let's sit with what happens when you don't align on them first. You waste years. You build separate futures under the same roof. And worst of all, you start to see money as a zero-sum game—every dollar toward your partner's priority feels like a dollar stolen from yours.

That's not a budget problem. That's a relationship problem wearing a budget's clothing.

The fix starts with a conversation you've probably been avoiding. Not the surface-level "we should save more" talk. The real one: *what do you actually want your life to look like in ten years? Twenty? When you're too old to work?*

Most couples skip this because it feels indulgent. Impractical. You've got bills to pay *now*; who has time to daydream about some hypothetical future? But here's the truth: if you don't know where you're going, every financial decision is just a guess. You're budgeting in the dark, hoping you'll stumble toward something that resembles security.

That's exhausting. And it doesn't work.

When my partner and I finally had this conversation—years later than we should have—I made her go first. I didn't want to influence her answer. I wanted to know what she *actually* wanted, not what she thought I wanted to hear or what sounded reasonable.

She talked for twenty minutes.

She wanted a house, yes, but not just any house—one with enough space for her parents to move in eventually, because she knew they wouldn't be able to afford assisted living on their own. She wanted to work part-time by fifty, not because she hated her job, but because she wanted time to take art classes again, something she'd given up after college. She wanted to travel, but not backpack-Europe travel—she wanted to go somewhere warm every February because seasonal depression hit her hard and she was tired of just enduring it.

None of this was news, exactly. I'd heard pieces of it over the years. But I'd never heard her say it all at once, as a cohesive picture of a life she was trying to build. And when it was my turn, I realized how much of my own vision I'd kept vague, even to myself.

I wanted our loans gone, yeah. But deeper than that, I wanted to never feel trapped in a job I hated because we couldn't afford for me to leave. I wanted the option to say no. That mattered more to me than owning property or retiring early—it was about autonomy, not assets.

We didn't agree on everything. But for the first time, we actually *knew* what we were disagreeing about.

That conversation happened on a Sunday morning in our kitchen. Coffee going cold on the counter. Neither of us showered yet. It wasn't planned or formal—we didn't sit down with notebooks and a agenda. She'd made some offhand comment about a house listing she'd seen, and instead of changing the subject like I usually did, I asked, "Why does the house matter so much to you?"

And she told me. Really told me.

When she got to the part about her parents, her voice cracked a little. She'd been carrying this alone—the knowledge that they had almost nothing saved, that she'd likely be supporting them within the next decade, that every month she *wasn't* saving felt like she was failing them. I'd known her parents were in rough shape financially. I hadn't known she was lying awake at night doing math in her head, trying to figure out how to fit two more people into our future.

My turn felt smaller after that. Less urgent. But she listened the same way I had—like she was actually hearing it for the first time, even though I'd probably complained about feeling trapped at work a hundred times before. The difference was context. I wasn't just venting about a bad boss or a frustrating project. I was telling her what I was afraid of: being fifty-five, still in a job I'd outgrown, unable to leave because we'd built a life that required every cent of my income.

We sat there for another hour. Made a second pot of coffee. By the end, we had a list—handwritten on the back of an envelope because neither of us wanted to break the momentum by finding actual paper—of the things we both wanted badly enough to sacrifice for.

It wasn't a budget yet. But it was a shared destination.

Start there. Sit down—actually sit down, not during commercial breaks or while one of you is folding laundry—and ask each other: what does financial freedom look like to you?

Be specific. “I want to be comfortable” doesn’t count. Comfortable how? What does a Tuesday look like in that life? Where do you live? What do you do with your time? Who are you supporting, and how?

Write it down. Both of you. Don’t edit yourself to sound practical or mature. If you want to own a cabin in Montana, write that. If you want to fund your niece’s theater company, write that. If your dream is to never set an alarm clock again after age fifty-five, write it.

This isn’t a budget yet. It’s just honest.

Then compare notes. You’ll find overlap—most couples do. Maybe you both value experiences over things, or you both want to support your extended families, or you’re both motivated by the idea of leaving something behind. Those overlaps are your foundation. Build there first.

The differences are harder. This is where a lot of couples stall out, because one person’s dream feels like a direct threat to the other’s. Early retirement versus college savings. Aggressive mortgage payoff versus travel. Investing in a business versus keeping a safety net untouched.

Here’s what I don’t believe in: the idea that one person’s goal has to die so the other’s can live. That’s not compromise—it’s capitulation. And it breeds resentment faster than almost anything else in a marriage. Instead, you’re looking for ways both visions can coexist, even if they can’t both get top billing.

Take Sarah and Mark from the advisor’s office. Once they stopped being defensive—and it took a few days; Sarah didn’t speak to him the first night, just locked herself in their bedroom and cried—they actually mapped it out.

Sarah's college fund wasn't just about tuition. It was about her kids having options she didn't have, not graduating with six figures of debt like she did. She'd worked three jobs through undergrad, slept four hours a night, and still graduated owing $87,000. She was forty-two and still paying it off. She'd missed friendships, experiences, the whole formative college experience people talk about, because she'd been too exhausted to do anything but work and study. She didn't want that for her kids.

Mark's early retirement wasn't about leisure. It was about reclaiming time with family while he was still healthy, after watching his father work until seventy-two and die six months into retirement. His dad had plans—he and Mark's mom were going to take that trip to Ireland she'd been dreaming about since she was a girl. Never happened. Heart attack in the garage, three weeks after his last day of work. Mark was seventeen when that happened. He's forty-nine now, and he still thinks about it constantly.

Neither of those motivations was frivolous. But they'd been treating them like competing line items instead of complementary parts of the same life.

They started contributing to an "Ours" account—$650 a month, proportional to their incomes. Sarah made more, so her contribution was higher. They agreed that 60 percent would go toward the kids' 529 plans, because that was her higher priority and she was putting in more money. But Mark got veto power over any withdrawal that wasn't education-related—no raiding it for a car or a wedding or anything else, no matter how they rationalized it later.

The other 40 percent went into an index fund they both agreed to leave untouched until Mark turned fifty-five, at which point they'd reevaluate whether early retirement was actually feasible or if that money needed redirecting. Maybe by then the kids would be through college and they could shift everything toward Mark's goal. Maybe his career would take off and he wouldn't want to retire early anymore. Maybe Sarah's parents would need help and the whole plan would have to flex.

The point wasn't to predict the future perfectly. It was to move in the same direction.

It wasn't perfect. It didn't make either of them entirely happy. Sarah still wished they were putting more toward college. Mark still felt like fifty-five was too far away, that he was gambling with time he might not have. But they were pulling together for the first time in a decade, and that mattered more than either of them expected.

Let me be clear: I don't believe in 50/50 splits. I think they're mathematically fair and emotionally bankrupt. Proportional contribution is the only approach that respects both partners' autonomy and acknowledges that "equal" and "fair" aren't the same thing.

If one person makes $80,000 and the other makes $45,000, they shouldn't both be dumping $500 a month into the Ours account—that's a wildly different sacrifice for each of them. For the $80,000 earner, $500 is about 7.5 percent of their gross monthly income. For the $45,000 earner, it's over 13 percent. That's not equal. That's not even close.

Calculate it as a percentage of income. If you decide that 10 percent of your combined income should go toward shared long-term goals, then the higher earner contributes 10 percent of *their* income, and the lower earner contributes 10 percent of *theirs*. It scales. It flexes when income changes. And it keeps both people invested without bankrupting the lower earner or making the higher earner feel like they're carrying the whole load alone.

Some couples balk at this. They want everything split evenly because it feels simpler, cleaner. But simple isn't always fair, and clean isn't always sustainable. You're not roommates splitting rent. You're partners building a life. Treat it like that.

Now: what do you actually *do* with the Ours account once it exists?

This is where most people stall. They set up the account, automate the transfers, feel virtuous for about two weeks, and then let it sit there accumulating like some vague promise of future security. But vague doesn't get you anywhere. You need targets.

Concrete, specific, prioritized targets.

Start by listing your big-picture goals—the ones you talked about earlier. Retirement, sure. But *what kind* of retirement? Do you want to travel six months a year, or downsize to a cabin and live simply? Are you planning to support aging parents, or leave an inheritance, or fund a passion project you've been putting off for twenty years?

Beyond retirement: what are the major expenses you see coming? A house down payment. A business launch. A sabbatical for grad school. College tuition—not just "college," but a specific number based on in-state public versus private, or trade school, or whatever your kids might actually need. The more specific you are now, the less you'll be guessing later.

Then rank them.

You can't fund everything at once, and pretending you can just leads to scattered progress and nothing fully funded. This is the hard part, because what feels absolutely essential to one partner might feel optional to the other.

Here's one method that worked for my partner and me: score each goal individually on a scale of one to five, based on importance *to you*. Not importance in general, not what sounds responsible—just what matters to you personally. Then share your scores and average them.

It's not perfect. It doesn't resolve fundamental disagreements. But it gives you a shared reference point. When college savings scores a 4.5 and early retirement scores a 3, you know where to focus first. You're not ignoring retirement; you're just being honest about sequencing.

Let me give you a real example—not Sarah and Mark this time, but another couple I know. David's fifty-two, Emily's forty-nine. One kid, age fourteen. They make about $140,000 combined and have almost nothing saved beyond a small emergency fund because they spent their thirties digging out of debt—medical bills from a pregnancy complication, credit cards they'd racked up in their early twenties when neither of them had any idea how money worked, a car loan that went underwater when David totaled the car two years in.

When they finally sat down to prioritize, David's list looked like this: early retirement (5), college fund (4), paying off the mortgage (3), travel (2), home renovation (1).

Emily's: college fund (5), secure retirement at a normal age (4), paying off their last student loan (3), regular family vacations (2), maybe some real estate investment down the line (1).

Averaged out: college fund (5 for both, so top priority). Retirement somewhere between early and standard (4.5 average, so second). Mortgage versus student loan payoff (tied at 3). Travel (2). Everything else (1).

They decided to put $1,500 a month into their Ours account—proportional to their incomes, so Emily contributed about $820 and David contributed $680. $700 went to the kid's 529 plan. $600 went to their retirement accounts, split between Emily's employer match and David's Roth IRA. The remaining $200 alternated monthly: one month to the mortgage, one month to knocking out that last student loan.

It wasn't elegant. But it was movement. Real, trackable progress toward things they both cared about.

And here's the part that mattered most: they reviewed it every quarter. Not because the plan was fragile, but because life isn't static.

Three months in, David's hours got cut during a slow season at work. His income dropped by about 20 percent. They adjusted—he dropped his Ours contribution temporarily to $480, Emily picked up the difference to keep them at $1,500 total. It wasn't charity. It was keeping them on track toward goals they'd agreed on together.

Six months later, Emily got a small raise. They didn't just automatically bump up the Ours contributions. They asked: is this the right move, or is there something else this money should do first? Turned out Emily had been quietly stressed about her own emergency fund—the "mine" account we talked about in earlier chapters. The raise gave her a chance to build that up without feeling like she was shortchangaging their shared goals. So they increased the Ours contributions by $100, but the bulk of her raise went toward her own financial security.

A year in, their kid decided he wanted to study music. That meant private lessons now—$180 a month—and maybe conservatory later, a whole different cost structure than they'd planned for. They didn't panic. They looked at the plan and adjusted. Dropped the mortgage/student loan alternating payment for six months while they figured out if the music thing was serious or a phase. When it became clear he was committed—he practiced without being nagged, started composing his own pieces, talked about music programs at colleges they couldn't afford—they reworked the college fund estimate and shifted more money there.

That's the system. It's not sexy. But it works.

Here's the framework, if you want something reusable.

Each of you lists your top five long-term financial goals. Be specific. Not "retirement"—"retire at sixty with enough passive income to cover basic expenses and travel internationally twice a year."

Score each goal from one to five based on how important it is to you personally. Don't strategize. Don't try to guess what your partner wants or what sounds more responsible. Just be honest.

Share your lists. Average the scores. See where you align and where you don't.

For each prioritized goal, estimate what it'll actually cost. Ballpark is fine—you're not trying to predict the future down to the dollar, just get a sense of scale. College might be $150,000 in today's money. A house down payment might be $60,000. Retirement might require a nest egg of seven figures to generate the income you want. (Talk to an actual financial advisor for retirement numbers—online calculators are fine for rough estimates, but they can't account for your specific situation.)

Decide how much you'll contribute to the Ours account each month. I'd suggest a percentage of your combined income—somewhere between 10 and 20 percent if you can swing it, but even 5 percent is better than nothing. Make it proportional: if you're aiming for 15 percent combined, each partner contributes 15 percent of their own income.

Allocate that monthly contribution across your top goals based on the priority ranking. The highest-ranked goal gets the biggest slice. You don't have to fund everything equally—in fact, you shouldn't. Concentrate your resources where they'll make the most impact.

Review quarterly. Life changes. Incomes shift. Priorities evolve. That's normal. The plan isn't supposed to be static—it's supposed to flex with you.

Let's talk about what happens when income changes mid-plan, because it will. Someone gets promoted. Someone loses a job. Someone decides to go back to school or take a sabbatical or care for a family member full-time.

When my partner got a significant raise a few years ago, we didn't just automatically bump up our Ours account contributions. We could have. It would've been easy. But we sat down and asked: is this the right move, or is there something else this money should do first?

Turns out, she'd been quietly stressed about her lack of personal savings—her mine account was basically nonexistent because every spare dollar had been going toward the house fund or my loan payments or our shared goals. The raise gave her a chance to build that up without feeling like she was shortchanging us. So we increased the Ours contributions, yeah, but modestly. The bulk of her raise went toward her own financial security, which ultimately made her a more confident, less anxious partner.

That was worth more than an extra $200 a month in the college fund.

On the flip side, when I had a contract fall through and lost about 30 percent of my expected income for a quarter, we didn't just shrug and let the Ours account drain. We adjusted. I dropped my contribution temporarily, and she picked up a bit more of the slack—not to cover me, but to keep us on track toward the goals we'd agreed on. When my income stabilized, we rebalanced. It wasn't a big deal because we'd built flexibility into the system from the start.

Here's the mistake I see couples make: they treat income changes like personal failures instead of just... information. Someone loses a job or takes a pay cut, and suddenly they're apologizing, or overcompensating, or withdrawing from financial conversations altogether because they feel like they're not holding up their end.

That's not partnership. Partnership is adjusting the plan when the variables change, without shame or scorekeeping.

If one partner's income drops significantly—or disappears entirely—you recalibrate. Maybe you reduce Ours account contributions across the board for a few months. Maybe the higher earner temporarily takes on a larger share, with the understanding that it'll rebalance later. Maybe you shift priorities: college savings can wait a few months, but keeping the mortgage paid can't.

The key is transparency. If you're the one whose income changed, say so. Don't try to quietly juggle it on your own, draining your personal account to maintain your contribution level while your partner has no idea you're struggling. And if you're the partner whose income stayed steady, don't treat the conversation like an interrogation. You're solving a logistics problem together, not assigning blame.

There's a bigger question lurking under all of this, and I'm just going to say it: what if one person consistently earns way more than the other? Not temporarily, but structurally. One partner's a surgeon making $350,000, the other's a teacher making $52,000. One's in tech pulling down $180,000, the other's a freelance artist lucky to clear $35,000 in a good year. The income gap isn't going anywhere.

This is where couples either get really honest or really resentful, and there's not much middle ground.

Proportional contributions help. They keep the lower earner from getting buried, from having to choose between contributing to shared goals and eating. But they don't erase the psychological weight of knowing you're contributing less in absolute terms, even if it's fair in relative terms. And they don't solve the power dynamics that can creep in when one person controls most of the resources.

I don't have a clean answer here. I wish I did. What I know is this: the Ours account only works if both people genuinely believe their contributions—financial *and* otherwise—are valued. If the higher earner starts keeping score, weaponizing their income in arguments or decision-making ("I'm paying for most of this house, so I get final say on renovations"), the whole system collapses. And if the lower earner starts feeling like a dependent instead of a partner, same result.

You have to talk about it. Explicitly. "Do you feel like your contributions matter, even though they're smaller in dollar terms?" "Do I ever make you feel like I'm carrying us financially?"

These are uncomfortable questions. Ask them anyway.

And recognize that contributions aren't just financial. If one partner's working sixty-hour weeks to bring in a big salary while the other's working thirty hours and handling most of the household labor and childcare, those are both contributions. The budget doesn't capture that, but your partnership has to.

I know a couple—she's a lawyer, he's a stay-at-home dad. She makes $240,000. He makes zero. Their Ours account is funded entirely by her income, but they treat it as equally theirs because they both agreed that him staying home with their two kids was worth more than the $60,000 he might make if he went back to his old project management job. More than the money, even. Worth her sanity, worth the kids actually being raised by a parent instead of a rotation of babysitters and after-school programs, worth him being the one to see their daughter's first steps and hear their son's first word.

They still argue about money sometimes. She still feels the weight of being the sole earner, the fear that if she loses her job or burns out, the whole family's sunk. He still feels weird about not contributing financially, even though they've agreed a hundred times that what he's doing matters. But they talk about it. They check in. They don't let it fester.

That's the work.

One more thing, because I keep seeing couples miss this: the Ours account isn't a restriction. It's not about locking your money away where you can't touch it or enjoy it. It's about making sure that *some* of your resources are consciously, deliberately directed toward the future you both want, instead of just drifting into whatever happens.

You can still take vacations. Buy things you want. Live your life now. But you're doing it with intention, not as a default. You're not spending everything that's left over after bills and hoping it'll somehow work out. You're deciding, together, how much goes toward today and how much goes toward tomorrow.

That's the shift. And it's harder than it sounds, because most of us were never taught to think this way. We were taught to avoid debt, maybe save for emergencies, and hope for the best. Nobody taught us how to align our financial lives with our actual values, or how to have these conversations without them turning into fights.

But this is the work. Not just setting up an account and automating transfers—that's easy. The work is the ongoing negotiation, the quarterly reviews, the willingness to adjust when life changes, the vulnerability of naming what you actually want and trusting your partner to care about it.

Sarah and Mark, from the advisor's office? They're doing okay now. Last I heard, they'd been funding their Ours account for almost three years. The college fund's in decent shape—not where Sarah wishes it was, but solid enough that she's stopped lying awake running worst-case scenarios. Mark's early retirement fund is growing slower than he'd like, but it's growing. And they're talking about taking a real vacation next summer, something they haven't done since before the kids were born.

They still don't agree on everything. Mark still wishes they were saving more aggressively for his early-out; Sarah still worries the college fund isn't growing fast enough. But they're having the same argument now instead of two different ones. They're pulling in the same direction, even when they disagree about the pace.

That matters more than the account balance.

Here's what I want you to do this week. Not next month. Not when you get your finances "in order" first. This week.

Sit down with your partner. Ask them what they want their life to look like in twenty years. Then tell them what you want yours to look like. Write it down. Both of you.

You don't have to solve everything in one conversation. You don't have to set up the account or run the numbers or figure out the perfect allocation. Just start with the conversation you've been avoiding.

Because here's what I've learned after years of doing this wrong and then slowly, painfully, learning to do it better: the couples who make it aren't the ones who never disagree about money. They're the ones who've figured out how to disagree toward the same destination. They're building different versions of the same future, not separate futures under the same roof.

The Ours account is just a tool. The real work is deciding what "ours" even means—what you're building together, what you're willing to sacrifice for, what you want badly enough to actually coordinate around instead of just hoping it works out.

You're going to disagree. Your priorities will shift. Life will throw you curveballs that make your careful plans look ridiculous in hindsight. That's fine. That's normal.

But you have to start with the conversation. The rest is just logistics.

Chapter 9: Putting It All Together: Your Couples Budgeting Blueprint

I still remember the night my partner and I had our worst money fight. We'd been together three years, living together for one, and we were sitting at our kitchen table with a pile of credit card statements between us. She'd just discovered I'd spent $600 on guitar pedals I didn't need. I'd just discovered she'd booked a weekend trip without telling me.

We weren't yelling—that would've been easier, honestly. We were just sitting there in this cold, awful silence, both thinking the same thing: *Maybe we're not as compatible as we thought.*

I remember looking at the pile of statements and feeling this specific flavor of dread I'd never experienced before. Not fear of poverty—we were both employed, reasonably stable. It was fear of incompatibility. Fear that the person I loved approached money in a way that was fundamentally at odds with how I approached it, and that no amount of love or good intentions would bridge that gap. That we could be perfect for each other in every other way and still end up destroying what we had because we couldn't figure out how to share a checking account without resenting each other.

That was eight years ago. We're married now, and we still have money disagreements, but they don't feel like relationship-enders anymore. The difference? We stopped trying to wing it. We built a system.

And look—I know what you're thinking. A *system* sounds rigid. Unromantic. The kind of thing that turns a relationship into a business partnership with shared health insurance. I thought the same thing. My wife did too, initially. She wanted us to just "be open with each other" and "communicate better," which are both great ideas and also completely insufficient when you're arguing about whether $200 on sneakers counts as a necessary expense or a luxury.

Here's what I learned: you can't communicate your way out of not having a framework. Communication without structure is just two people explaining their feelings really articulately while still having no idea how to actually split the electric bill.

This chapter is that system. Everything we've covered so far—the Mine/Ours split, proportional contributions, the monthly check-ins, the conversation frameworks—it all comes together here. Not into some complicated financial management software that requires a degree to operate, but into something simpler: a living agreement between two people who are trying to build a life together without destroying each other in the process.

Let me be direct about something. Most couples budgeting advice treats money like it's just math. Add up the income, subtract the expenses, split everything down the middle, done. That's garbage. Money is never just math. It's power, it's security, it's childhood wounds, it's dreams deferred and anxieties projected into the future. A 50/50 split might look fair on paper, but if one person makes $100,000 and the other makes $40,000, that "fairness" is just shared poverty for one partner and easy generosity for the other.

I don't believe in equal splits. I believe in proportional contribution based on income, because that's the only approach that respects both partners' autonomy while acknowledging that "equal" and "fair" aren't remotely the same thing.

The blueprint I'm about to walk you through isn't theoretical. It's built from watching hundreds of couples—including myself and my wife—navigate this exact territory. Some made it through. Some didn't. The ones who made it all had one thing in common: they formalized their financial partnership before crisis forced them to.

The Couples Financial Agreement: Your One-Page Constitution

Think about what happens without one.

You have vague conversations about money when you move in together. Maybe you agree that you'll both "contribute" to rent and groceries, whatever that means. Maybe you even get specific for a minute—you'll pay the rent, she'll pay utilities—but you don't write it down, don't revisit it, don't account for the fact that your income or circumstances might change. You just sort of... proceed.

And for a while, it works. Or seems to. Then six months in, one person realizes they're consistently broke at the end of every month while the other seems to have plenty left over for discretionary spending. But you don't say anything, because bringing it up feels petty or accusatory. So resentment builds. Quietly. Until it's not quiet anymore, and you're having a fight that isn't really about the $60 you spent on takeout last week—it's about six months of feeling like you're carrying an unfair burden while your partner skates by.

I watched this exact scenario play out with a couple I know—let's call them Alex and Jordan. Both in their late twenties, both employed, both reasonable people. They'd been living together for almost a year when Alex finally snapped over Jordan buying a $400 bike without "checking in first." The thing is, they'd never actually established that checking in was required. They'd never defined what amount of money constituted "big enough to discuss." They'd never formalized *anything*, just operated on a series of unstated assumptions that turned out to be completely different.

They broke up three months later. Not because either of them was irresponsible or cruel, but because they'd never built the infrastructure to handle normal financial friction, and by the time they tried, the resentment was too calcified to work through.

You need something tangible. Not a vague understanding or good intentions, but an actual document both of you sign and revisit regularly. I call it the Couples Financial Agreement, and yes, that sounds formal—intentionally so. Marriage is formal. Mortgages are formal. Why should the intersection of the two be handled with a handshake and crossed fingers?

This isn't a budget spreadsheet. Those are for tracking what happened. This is for deciding what *will* happen—before life gets messy and emotions run hot.

Here's how it works. One page, front and back. That's it.

Front side: The Core Framework

At the top, you write out your Mine/Ours percentages. Not just the numbers—the *reasoning* behind them. When you're six months in and one person is frustrated because they're broke while the other is flush, you need to remember why you agreed to these numbers in the first place.

Example:

Mine – 55% Covers individual discretionary spending, personal debt repayment, hobbies, gifts, clothing. Acknowledges that we value financial independence within partnership and that our spending styles differ—this prevents resentment over how the other person chooses to spend their personal allocation.

Ours – 45% Joint expenses: mortgage, utilities, groceries, household maintenance, insurance, streaming services, date nights, shared vacations. Savings for down payment on a house. Emergency fund contributions (target: 6 months expenses).

Notice what's happening here. It's not just categories and percentages. It's the *why*.

When David (who we met in Chapter 3) and his partner Elena first did this, Elena wrote under "Mine": "I need discretionary money for therapy and personal wellness spending that feels separate from our shared budget because asking permission for self-care makes me feel like I'm back living with my controlling parents."

That's real. That's the kind of honesty that makes this whole thing work. Not "therapy falls under Mine" but *why* it needs to fall under Mine, what it means emotionally for her to have that money ring-fenced from discussion or approval. David told me later that reading that line completely shifted how he thought about their budget. He'd been mildly annoyed that Elena wanted such a high Mine percentage, thought maybe she was just being selfish. Then he read that sentence and realized it wasn't about selfishness—it was about autonomy after growing up in a household where every dollar was controlled and monitored.

You might be thinking this level of disclosure feels vulnerable, maybe too vulnerable for a budget document. I get it. My wife and I had that exact conversation when we were filling ours out. She didn't want to put down that part of her Mine allocation was going toward student loans from a degree she never finished, because she felt embarrassed about it. I didn't want to admit that I was spending money on music equipment partly because I was still clinging to this fantasy of "making it" as a musician in my thirties, which felt pathetic to write down.

But here's the thing: the vulnerability is the point. If you can't be honest about *why* you need the money structured a certain way, you're just creating a prettier version of the same dysfunction. The couples I've seen make this work are the ones who got uncomfortable on purpose, early, when the stakes were still relatively low.

Below the percentages, you define your **Spending Thresholds**.

This is where most couples discover they have completely different internal calibrations for what constitutes a "big" purchase. What feels significant to you might not register for your partner, and vice versa. I once talked to a couple where one person thought anything over $30 required discussion, and the other thought the threshold should be $500. They'd been living together for two years and had never explicitly surfaced this gap—just assumed the other person shared their sense of what was "reasonable."

Some couples do a flat number: anything over $150 requires a conversation. Others use a tiered system:

- Under $50: automatic, no discussion needed - $50-$200: quick heads-up (text, mention at dinner, whatever) - Over $200: full conversation before committing

The specific numbers matter less than the agreement itself. I've seen couples set the threshold at $30 because they're on a tight budget and every dollar counts. I've seen others set it at $500 because they're both high earners and don't want to micromanage each other. Either works, as long as you both actually honor it.

And look—I still mess this up sometimes. Last month I bought a used synthesizer for $275 without texting my wife first because I convinced myself it was "basically a work expense" since I occasionally score short films. It wasn't, really. She wasn't mad, but she was annoyed, and she was right to be. Our threshold is $200. I crossed it. The system only works if you actually follow it, and I got lazy.

The thing is, even messing it up occasionally is fine as long as you acknowledge it and course-correct. What kills couples isn't the occasional slip—it's the refusal to admit there was a slip, or the pattern of repeatedly crossing agreed-upon lines and then getting defensive when called on it.

The last section on the front is **Check-In Frequency**. How often will you sit down together and review this entire agreement?

Quarterly is a solid starting point for most couples. More often than that and it feels like homework. Less often and you drift out of alignment without realizing it. My wife and I do ours on the first Saturday of March, June, September, and December. We put it in our calendar as a recurring event with a reminder, same as we would for a dentist appointment or a friend's birthday. Sounds unromantic, I know. But you know what's really unromantic? Discovering in month seven that your partner has been quietly furious about the budget for weeks and you had no idea.

Write it down. Put it in your calendar. Treat it like any other recurring appointment that actually matters.

Back side: When Things Go Wrong (Because They Will)

Flip the page over.

This is where you stop pretending everything will go smoothly and start planning for the inevitable disruptions: unexpected expenses, income changes, emergencies, disagreements. The couples who survive financial stress aren't the ones who avoid it—nobody avoids it—they're the ones who decided in advance how they'd handle it.

First section: **Triggers for Re-evaluation**

What circumstances would prompt you to revisit and potentially revise the Mine/Ours split? Not "whenever we feel like it"—that's too vague. Specific triggers:

- Either partner's income changes by more than 15% - Major life event: pregnancy, job loss, serious illness, move to a new city - Completion of a major savings goal (down payment saved, debt paid off) - Discovery that current split is consistently causing financial stress for one partner

These are forcing functions. They give you permission—actually, they give you a *requirement*—to renegotiate when circumstances change.

Too many couples stick with an outdated agreement because revisiting it feels awkward or confrontational. I know a couple who kept their original 50/50 split for three years after one partner's income nearly doubled, purely because neither of them wanted to be the one to bring up changing it. The lower earner felt embarrassed asking for an adjustment, like they were admitting they couldn't keep up. The higher earner felt guilty suggesting it, like they were rubbing their success in their partner's face. So they just... didn't. And the resentment compounded until it poisoned everything else.

Having triggers written into your agreement removes that barrier. "Hey, your income just went up 20%. According to our agreement, we need to talk about adjusting the split." Not an accusation. Just the system working as designed.

Next: **Emergency Fund Access**

How much do you have saved? Who can access it, under what circumstances, and how much can be withdrawn without needing the other person's sign-off?

Sarah and David (the teacher and freelance designer from earlier) had $5,000 in their emergency fund. They agreed that either partner could use up to $1,000 for a genuine emergency without needing immediate consultation—though they'd still discuss it within 24 hours. Anything over $1,000 required mutual agreement before the money got spent.

Why the $1,000 threshold? Because David's car had broken down twice in the past year—once the repair was $800, the other time $1,200—and they didn't want to be calling each other from the mechanic's shop trying to get permission to fix the car he needed to get to work. But they also didn't want one person unilaterally draining the fund on something that wasn't actually an emergency.

This is where you decide what "emergency" even means for the two of you. Is it just catastrophic stuff—medical bills, job loss, major home repairs? Or does it include smaller urgent needs like replacing a broken laptop you need for work? Define it now, before the pressure hits.

And crucially: **How will you replenish it?** If you pull $2,000 from the emergency fund, do you both immediately increase your "Ours" contributions for the next few months until it's back up to the target? Does it come entirely from the next windfall (tax refund, bonus, whatever)?

Spell it out. Because I've watched couples drain an emergency fund during a crisis and then just... never refill it. Six months later they're still operating without a safety net, telling themselves they'll get back to it eventually, and then the next emergency hits and suddenly they're going into debt because the fund they thought they had doesn't exist anymore.

Then the most important section on this whole page: **Disagreement Resolution**

You are going to disagree about money. It's not an if, it's a when and how often. So you need ground rules established when you're both calm and rational, not in the middle of a fight.

Think about the last major money argument you had with your partner. If you're like most couples, it probably escalated quickly. Someone said something slightly sharp, the other person got defensive, and within three minutes you were having a completely different fight about something that happened six months ago. The original issue—whether to spend $300 on new running shoes—became a referendum on who contributes more to the relationship and whose career is taken more seriously and who cares more about the future.

That's what happens without a circuit breaker built into the system.

Some couples write out full conflict-resolution protocols. Others keep it simple. Here's what my wife and I have written down:

1. **Either person can call a timeout if the conversation is escalating.** We use "pause" as the safe word. It's not about avoiding the issue—it's about preventing a productive discussion from turning into a damaging fight. When someone says "pause," we table it for at

least two hours, sometimes until the next day.

2. **Both people get to fully state their position without interruption.** We set a timer for three minutes each. Sounds artificial, but it works. It forces you to actually listen instead of just waiting for your turn to talk.

3. **We acknowledge that both perspectives are valid,** even when they're incompatible. This is huge. It's not about one person being right and the other being wrong—it's about two different sets of needs and values that both matter.

4. **If we can't reach agreement within one conversation, we revisit it in three days.** Most of the time, some distance gives us perspective we didn't have in the heat of the moment.

Write down your own rules. Maybe yours involve a mediator friend you both trust. Maybe it's a commitment to never discuss money after 9 PM because you're both tired and cranky by then. Whatever works for your specific dynamic.

The point isn't to have the perfect system—it's to have *a* system that you both agree to follow when things get heated.

And one more thing that might sound unnecessary but I promise you it's not: include a section for **Appreciation & Celebration**. When you hit a savings goal, when you successfully navigate a tough financial month, when one person makes a sacrifice for the shared good—acknowledge it.

Write down how you'll celebrate: a nice dinner out, a weekend trip, whatever feels meaningful. Financial partnership shouldn't be all stress and restriction. Build in the rewards, or the whole thing starts to feel like deprivation and you'll unconsciously sabotage it just to get some relief.

Making It Real: Sarah and David's Blueprint

Let me show you what this looks like in practice.

Sarah and David—both earning around $60,000 annually, but with wildly different spending styles—spent about two hours on a Saturday morning filling out their Couples Financial Agreement. They sat at their kitchen table with coffee and the framework I've just described, and they actually did the work.

Not in some half-hearted "let's just get through this" way, but really engaged with it. Sarah told me later that the first thirty minutes were awkward as hell. They kept making jokes to diffuse the tension, kept trying to skip over the "why" sections because writing them out felt too exposing. But they pushed through.

They landed on a 55/45 split: 55% to Mine, 45% to Ours.

Sarah's "Mine" reasoning: "Allows me flexibility for creative workshops and travel essential for my business development as a freelance designer, plus some buffer for irregular income months."

David's: "Covers my woodworking hobby, which I'm trying to turn into a side income stream, plus student loan payments that are mine alone."

Notice they didn't just write "personal spending." They got specific about *why* their Mine allocations needed to be what they were. Sarah needed buffer room because freelance income is unpredictable. David needed to service debt that pre-dated the relationship. Both legitimate, both different.

Their threshold: $100. Anything over that required discussion.

Sarah initially wanted it at $200, David wanted $50. They compromised, and David admitted later he was glad they didn't go with his number because it would've felt suffocating. He'd grown up in a household where every purchase was scrutinized, and part of what he loved about being an adult with his own income was the freedom to buy a $75 chisel set without having to justify it to anyone. Setting the threshold at $50 would've triggered that old anxiety.

On the back of their worksheet: Income change trigger was set at 10% because Sarah's freelance income fluctuated. Emergency fund target was $10,000 (they had $5,000 saved when they started). Either could access up to $1,000 without consultation. Replenishment plan: any tax refund goes directly to emergency fund until it hits target, then splits according to Mine/Ours percentages.

Their disagreement resolution rule: "We each state our needs calmly and acknowledge the validity of the other's perspective. If we're getting heated, either person can say 'bluebird' and we pause for at least two hours."

Why bluebird? Sarah loved birds. It was meaningful to her, which made it effective. The word itself doesn't matter—what matters is having it agreed upon in advance, something specific and a little absurd so it cuts through the heat of the moment.

They printed it out, stuck it on their fridge with a magnet, and—this is the crucial part—they actually revisited it every quarter.

The first three months were rocky. David went over his "Mine" budget by $400, mostly on woodworking tools he convinced himself were investments. Sarah felt resentful that she was sticking to the plan while he wasn't. They had a tense check-in where Sarah said "bluebird" twice because she could feel herself getting angry.

But they worked through it. David agreed to sell some of the tools he wasn't using and put that money back. They adjusted the budget to give him a bit more space for the hobby, but with the understanding that if it didn't start generating income within six months, they'd revisit again.

It did—he started selling cutting boards and small furniture pieces, bringing in an extra $300-400 a month, which went straight to their house down payment fund. Sarah told me that watching David actually follow through on the "turn it into income" promise completely shifted her feelings about the tools. It stopped feeling like frivolous spending and started feeling like an investment in their shared future.

Two years in, Sarah got a big contract that bumped her income up by 30% for four months. According to their agreement, that triggered a re-evaluation. They temporarily adjusted to 50/50 during those high-earning months, banking the extra into their down payment fund. When the contract ended and her income normalized, they went back to 55/45. No drama, no resentment, just the system working.

That's what this blueprint does. It doesn't eliminate disagreements—that's a fantasy. It gives you a structure for navigating them without each fight feeling like it might end the relationship.

The Emergency Conversation Starter Kit

Even with the agreement in place, you still need to know how to actually *talk* about money without it turning into a fight. The blueprint tells you what to discuss and when; this part is about *how*.

First, language matters more than you think.

"You always overspend on restaurants" is an attack. "I've noticed our dining-out category is over budget this month—can we talk about how to adjust that?" is an opening. The difference is subtle but massive. One puts the other person on the defensive. The other invites collaboration.

Same with "You don't care about our future" versus "I feel anxious when we're not saving as much as we planned. Can we look at where the money's going and see if we can redirect some of it?" One's an accusation about character. The other's a feeling and a request.

I'm not naturally good at this, for what it's worth. My default mode in conflict is to get sarcastic and passive-aggressive, which my wife finds infuriating (correctly). I've had to actively train myself to use "I feel" statements instead of "You always" statements, and I still screw it up regularly. But even imperfectly applied, it helps.

The other thing that saves us regularly: having a pre-agreed pause signal that we honor immediately, no questions asked.

Last year we were arguing about whether to replace our aging couch. I thought it was fine for another year or two and wanted to put the money toward a vacation. She thought it was embarrassing and wanted to replace it now. We were going in circles, voices getting sharper, when she said "pause."

I wanted to keep arguing—I was on a roll, had some great points lined up—but we'd agreed that "pause" was non-negotiable. So we stopped. Went to separate rooms. Came back two hours later, and I immediately saw her point in a way I'd been too defensive to see during the argument. We compromised: cheaper couch than she wanted, sooner than I wanted. Both of us slightly dissatisfied, which probably means it was the right call.

Here's a few more conversation openers that work:

Instead of "Why did you spend so much on [thing]?" try "Help me understand what you were thinking with [purchase]."

Instead of "We can't afford this," try "I'm worried about how this fits into our budget—can we look at the numbers together?"

Instead of "You never stick to the budget," try "I've noticed we're consistently over in [category]. What's going on there?"

The pattern: move from accusation to curiosity, from "you're doing it wrong" to "help me understand."

Common Financial Flashpoints (And How to Navigate Them)

Let's talk about specific scenarios that trip up even couples with good systems in place.

Income Disparity: One person makes $120,000, the other makes $45,000.

The temptation is to split everything 50/50 because that feels "fair," but it's not. It's financially crippling for the lower earner and creates a power imbalance that corrodes the relationship. Proportional contribution is the only approach that works. If your combined income is $165,000, the higher earner contributes about 73% of shared expenses, the lower earner about 27%. Then each person has similar discretionary money left over relative to their lifestyle.

I've seen so many couples resist this because the higher earner feels like they're "paying for" the other person. That's the wrong frame. You're not paying for your partner. You're both contributing to a shared life in a way that doesn't force one person into poverty while the other lives comfortably.

If you can't get on board with that mindset, you probably shouldn't be combining finances at all. Because what's the alternative? Your partner consistently struggles to make ends meet while you enjoy financial comfort, and you tell yourself that's "fair" because you're splitting things equally? That's not partnership. That's just two people who happen to share a mailing address.

The Unexpected Expense Bomb: Car repair, medical bill, broken furnace.

These will happen. The emergency fund handles it if you've built one. If you haven't, you're about to go into debt or raid savings meant for something else, which derails your long-term goals and breeds resentment.

I remember when our water heater died on a Sunday night in January. $1,800 to replace it, couldn't wait, no choice. We had the emergency fund. Wrote the check, scheduled the install, moved on. If we hadn't had that fund, we would've been scrambling—putting it on a credit card we couldn't pay off, arguing about whose "fault" it was that we didn't have savings, probably fighting about money for the next three weeks.

When these hit and the emergency fund doesn't fully cover it, you have to revisit the budget immediately, together. Not "I'll handle it" from one partner. Both of you, looking at the numbers, deciding where to cut back temporarily. Maybe you postpone a non-essential purchase. Maybe you eat out less for two months. Maybe you both pick up a freelance gig or sell some stuff you don't need. The key is shared sacrifice, not one person bearing the burden alone.

Job Loss: This is the worst-case scenario, and it requires immediate action and total transparency.

First step: take a deep breath and don't panic. Panic makes you do stupid things like draining your retirement account or putting everything on credit cards at high interest rates.

Second step: Emergency household meeting. Full honesty about the financial situation. How much savings? How much can you cut from the budget immediately? What are the non-negotiable expenses?

My wife lost her job four years ago—tech company layoff, not performance-related, but it still felt like a gut punch. We sat down that night and went through everything.

We cut our "Ours" spending by about 40%: paused streaming services except one, stopped eating out entirely, put the vacation fund on hold. We also contacted our mortgage lender about a temporary forbearance program (didn't end up needing it, but knowing it was available reduced the panic). She filed for unemployment immediately. Within three weeks she had freelance work coming in. Two months later she had a new full-time job, better than the one she'd lost.

But if we hadn't had the emergency fund, hadn't had a clear budget we could quickly revise, hadn't had the relationship foundation to have hard conversations without blame—it would've been so much worse. The financial system we'd built didn't prevent the job loss, but it contained the damage.

Control Issues: If one person manages all the finances and the other is kept in the dark, that's not partnership.

That's a recipe for resentment and financial abuse. Even if one person handles the day-to-day tracking, both partners need full visibility and equal say in major decisions. Monthly check-ins aren't optional. They're how you prevent power imbalances from calcifying.

I know a couple where one person handled "all the money stuff" for years while the other just trusted them. Worked fine until it didn't—turned out the person managing everything had run up significant credit card debt that the other partner knew nothing about. By the time it came out, they were $30,000 in the hole and the relationship was basically over. Not because of the debt itself, but because of the secrecy, the unilateral decisions, the complete violation of trust.

Life Transitions: Baby, career change, move, going back to school.

These all require budget overhauls. Don't wait until you're in the middle of the transition to figure out how you'll handle it financially.

When my wife and I started talking about having kids, we spent three months running different budget scenarios before she got pregnant. What would our expenses look like with childcare? Could we afford for one of us to go part-time? How much parental leave could we handle financially? We mapped it all out, adjusted our savings strategy, built up a bigger buffer.

Then she got pregnant and all our careful planning went partially out the window because life is messy and babies are expensive in ways you can't fully anticipate. But having done the planning meant we had a baseline to work from, a framework to adjust rather than building from scratch while sleep-deprived and overwhelmed.

The "It's My Money" Problem: This comes up most often when one person brings significant assets into the relationship or receives an inheritance or major windfall.

The question becomes: is this "ours" or "mine"? And the answer depends entirely on what you've agreed to in advance. I know couples where an inheritance went entirely into the recipient's Mine account. I know others where it went straight into Ours. Both can work, as long as it's discussed and decided together, not assumed.

The worst version I've seen: one partner inherited $80,000 from a grandparent, put it all in a personal account without discussing it, and then got furious when the other partner questioned why they were still splitting expenses 50/50 when one person was sitting on a pile of money. The inheritor felt like their partner was being grabby and entitled. The partner felt like they were being excluded from a major financial development that affected both their lives. Neither was entirely wrong, but they'd never established the rules for how to handle it.

Starting from Here, Not from Perfect

Maybe you're reading this and thinking: we're already years into our relationship, already have bad habits established, already have resentment built up. Is it too late?

No. But it's going to be harder.

You can't implement this blueprint and expect all the existing tension to vanish. You're going to have to acknowledge the ways the old system (or lack of system) failed you both, probably apologize for your part in it, definitely have some uncomfortable conversations about what needs to change going forward.

When I've worked with couples trying to implement this after years of financial dysfunction, the biggest hurdle is usually resistance from whoever benefits from the status quo. If you've been keeping one partner in the dark about finances, you're going to have to give up that control. If you've been free-riding on your partner's higher income without contributing proportionally, you're going to have to step up. If you've been avoiding money conversations by just putting everything on credit cards and hoping it works out, you're going to have to face the reality of your situation.

It's not comfortable. But neither is staying in a relationship where money is a constant source of conflict and resentment.

Start with one piece. Maybe just the spending threshold conversation. See if you can agree on a number and honor it for one month. Then add the quarterly check-in. Then the Mine/Ours split. Build the system incrementally if doing it all at once feels overwhelming.

The couples I've seen successfully turn things around are the ones who treated it like a genuine reset—acknowledged that the old way wasn't working, committed to trying a new way even if it felt awkward or formal, and gave themselves permission to adjust as they went.

Your agreement doesn't have to be perfect. It has to be *explicit*. Documented. Revisited regularly. Adjusted when circumstances change.

That's it. That's the whole system.

You write down how you're going to handle money together. You follow what you wrote. When it stops working, you revise it together. You don't wing it, don't assume, don't operate on unstated expectations and then get mad when your partner doesn't meet them.

Most relationship advice tells you to "communicate better," which is fine but insufficient. This is giving you something specific to communicate *about*, a framework to communicate *within*, and a regular cadence to make sure the communication actually happens instead of only occurring during crisis.

Will it prevent every money fight? No. Will it make the fights you do have more productive and less damaging? Yes.

Will it guarantee your relationship survives every financial challenge? No. Will it give you the best possible shot at navigating those challenges together instead of letting them drive you apart? Yes.

The blueprint doesn't create compatibility where none exists. But if you're fundamentally compatible and money is just the thing that keeps getting in the way—this is how you remove that obstacle.

Also in the Series

Every book in Money Reset stands on its own — read them in any order. If this one was useful, the library continues:

Tax Strategies to Keep What You Earn

Salary Negotiation Before You Sign

Budgeting for People Who Hate Budgeting

Budgeting From Zero

Budgeting on an Irregular Income

Budgeting After Debt

Budgeting for the Broke Paycheck

Budgeting Without a Spreadsheet

Budgeting for Impulse Spending

Budgeting for a Bigger Life

www.ingramcontent.com/pod-product-compliance
Lightning Source LLC
LaVergne TN
LVHW010730061126
851857LV00014B/1423